Is There Really Sex After Kids?

Other books in the
Hearts at Home Workshop Series

Professionalizing Motherhood by Jill Savage
Becoming a Chief Home Officer by Allie Plieter

Is There Really

A MOM-TO-MOM CHAT ON KEEPING INTIMACY ALIVE

Sex After Kids?

JILL SAVAGE
FOUNDER AND DIRECTOR OF HEARTS AT HOME®

WITH LEADER'S GUIDE AND PERSONAL REFLECTIONS

ZONDERVAN™

GRAND RAPIDS, MICHIGAN 49530 USA

Is There Really Sex After Kids?
Copyright © 2003 by Jill Savage

Requests for information should be addressed to:

Zondervan, *Grand Rapids, Michigan 49530*

Library of Congress Cataloging-in-Publication Data

Savage, Jill, 1964–
  Is there really sex after kids? : a mom-to-mom chat on keeping intimacy alive /
by Jill Savage.
     p. cm. – (Hearts at home workshop series)
  ISBN 0-310-23743-2
  1. Marriage — Religious aspects — Christianity. 2. Sex — Religious aspects —
Christianity. I. Title. II. Series.
BV835.S38 2003
248.8'435 — dc21

2002154457

Published in association with Yates & Yates, LLP, Attorneys and Counselors, Suite
1000, Literary Agent, Orange, CA.

Interior design by Susan Ambs

Printed in the United States of America

03 04 05 06 07/❖ DC/ 10 9 8 7 6 5 4 3 2 1

contents

∽

Acknowledgments

WITH SPECIAL THANKS:

To all of the Hearts at Home staff. You are my friends and co-laborers in ministry. Thank you for your commitment to the profession of motherhood and thank you for the encouragement you gave me during this project. I do love your creative title ideas for this book; however, *Savage Sex* and *Sex the Savage Way* are indeed my favorites!

To my friends and family who pored over manuscripts: Mike and Becky, Holly, Beth, Cathy, Mary, and Julie. Your input and honesty helped me greatly.

To Angie. Thank you for your research and assistance in this project.

To Larry and Laurie, who let me use their cabin as a writing getaway. Thank you for sharing your beautiful home with me again.

To my friends Irene, Julie, Cathy, and Nancy, who helped with kids, carpooling, and anything else that needed to be done in the midst of book deadlines. Thank you to all my dear friends, whom I can't possibly name, who prayed, encouraged, and helped in a variety of ways.

To my prayer team and our Crosswinds Community Church family: Thank you for spending time on your knees for me.

To Dr. Harold Nord, M.D.; Crystal Smith, R.N., C.S., M.S.N., F.N.P.; and Dr. Mark Gentry, M.D. Your medical insight was invaluable to my research process.

To Cindy Hays and Sue Brower of Zondervan, for catching the vision of Hearts at Home and helping to make this project a reality!

To Angela Scheff, my Zondervan editor. You have done a wonderful job helping to make this book the best it can be. It has been a privilege to work with you.

To Sealy and Susan Yates, my literary agents. Thank you for believing in the ministry of Hearts at Home.

Your help in making published resources available to mothers at home across the world means so much to me.

To my sister-in-law, Denise. Thank you for your words of encouragement.

To my sisters, Jackie and Juli. Thank you for your encouragement.

To my parents, Duane and Patsy Fleener. Thank you for your example of a loving marriage relationship. Can you believe your daughter really wrote a book about sex?

To my grandma, Annabelle Chambers. Thank you for your love and support.

To my children, Anne, Evan, Erica, and Austin, who were willing to eat a few more frozen pizzas than usual during the writing deadlines. Someday you'll be able to understand the importance of the message of this book when you are married and have children of your own. Until then … no you can't read the book yet.

To my dear husband, Mark, who is my teammate, my confidante, my best friend, and my coauthor. Thank you for supporting me in this ministry adventure and sharing your insights with the husbands of the women who will read this book. I love you!

To Jesus Christ, my Lord and Savior, for loving me, saving me, and equipping me. Thank you for the incredible gift of sex. And thank you, Lord, for your words, your Truth, and your direction both in the ministry of Hearts at Home and during this writing project.

Helpful Features of This Book

Personal Reflection Questions

These questions and reflection points, found at the end of each chapter, allow the reader to apply the chapter's principles to her personal life. They take the concepts one step further—from information to transformation.

For Husbands Only

These short, easy-to-read messages at the end of every chapter are from Jill's husband, Mark. They have a two-fold purpose. First, they allow the couple to "read" the book together. While she may be reading the bulk of the material, he gets the condensed version of the same topics discussed in each chapter. Second, they represent the male perspective on a subject that intertwines the heart, mind, and body of every married couple.

Leader's Guide

This section helps both the novice and the experienced leader facilitate discussion and move a group beyond comprehension to application. The four-part session design features an icebreaker, questions that dig deep and bring energy to a discussion, and application assignments that help drive the principles home. The discussion closes with a focus on prayer.

How to Use This Book

As an Individual Woman

Jill's personal style makes reading the book feel like sitting down and having a cup of coffee with a friend. The Personal Reflection Questions at the end of each chapter allow for further application of the principles discussed in each chapter.

As a Couple

This book features encouragement for both husband and wife. Assuming the primary reader is female, Jill shares with wives insights, anecdotes, and helps. Her husband, Mark, offers a quick read for husbands at the end of the chapter. This allows the couple to discuss the information in the book and how it applies to their relationship.

As a Moms' Group Study

The design of this book lends itself to being used as curriculum for moms' groups. Mothers can read a chapter at home before the group meets. The leader's guide in the back of the book will assist the person leading the group discussion.

As a Sunday School or Small Group Study for Couples

While the book is certainly written with a female audience in mind, it can easily be read by both men and women. Discussion will be fostered by helps in the leader's guide at the end of the book.

I Can't Believe I'm Writing
a Book About Sex!

"HI, I'M JILL SAVAGE. My husband, Mark, and I have been married nineteen years, nine of them happily." This is the way I usually introduce myself when speaking to women's groups on the topic of marriage. Our marriage was a mess during the first ten years. It was a mess we both created by our selfishness, anger, pride, and criticism. The fact that neither one of us really knew *how* to be married greatly contributed to our shipwrecked relationship.

Shortly after our seventh anniversary, Mark and I sought help. We saw a marriage counselor and sought out resources that would help us learn how to be married. We read books, attended seminars, and began to make the necessary changes to make this relationship go the distance.

Our sexual relationship was an even bigger mess. Part of the counseling we received was sexual counseling, and we searched for resources to help us understand sexual intimacy in marriage. At that time, I couldn't have cared less about sex. I was knee deep in diapers and dishes. Making meat loaf was a higher priority than making love.

I eventually shared openly about our marriage struggles in the moms' group I led. My honesty opened the doors to more transparency within the group. I soon discovered Mark and I were not the only ones dealing with difficulties in marriage.

I found myself fielding many questions from other moms concerning marriage and sexual intimacy. Most of these questions would be asked over a cup of coffee with small children playing at our feet. Over time, I saw a pattern to the questions being asked, "What does God think about sex?" "What is okay and what is not okay in bed?" "What do I do when his desire is sky-high and mine is non-existent?" "Is there really sex after kids?"

The teacher in me saw the need to address this with our entire moms' group. I was just beginning to grasp a new understanding of marriage and sexual intimacy myself. However, I've always been one to pass something along as soon as I've learned it. This topic was no different.

The first time I presented a discussion on sexual intimacy, the women were extremely appreciative. There was an incredible thirst for God's perspective on marriage and the sexual relationship.

Eventually, I presented the "sex workshop" at a Hearts at Home conference. When almost 25 percent of the 5,000 women selected this workshop as their top choice, we knew we were meeting a felt need. In the past four years, this has become my most requested speaking topic for churches and moms' groups.

The book you now hold in your hands is a result of hundreds of workshops and years of mentoring couples with my husband, Mark, who is a pastor. Although I've certainly done my share of research in this process, I write primarily from my own experience as a wife and a mother.

You'll meet a lot of women in this book just like yourself. Please know that all names mentioned have been changed to protect those who talked with me honestly from their hearts. The only exceptions are references to friends Karen and Todd and Doris and Charlie, who are willing to have their names remain unchanged.

Would you like to learn more about God's beautiful gift of sex? Join me as we discover the fine art of pleasuring, learn more about the differences between men and women, and develop strategies that help you move from frustration to fascination. The expedition promises to deepen the intimacy you experience in your marriage.

Is there really sex after kids? Turn the page, and we'll start our journey to find the answer to that burning question!

The Plan—God Created Sex!

chapter 1

God Created Sex!

"SEX … I COULD GO the rest of my life without it!" I cried to my husband as we arrived back to the bed-and-breakfast we had reserved for a two-day marriage get-away. "I'm not interested. I have no desire. I'm too tired, and I can't seem to ever meet your needs!" were my responses to his request for intimacy. We had made arrangements for our two preschool children, Anne and Evan, to stay with friends for a few days so Mark and I could take some time for just the two of us. I had packed one of the few skimpy nightgowns I owned, but honestly hoped I could get through the weekend without wearing it. I didn't feel one bit of sexual desire in my body. After spending the past four years either pregnant or nursing, I couldn't even remember what it was like to be a lover.

Just days earlier we had had the same argument. As I stood at the kitchen sink washing the dinner dishes, Mark came up from behind and wrapped his arms around me. I stiffened at his embrace, knowing it was accompanied by expectations I didn't have any desire to meet. After we put the kids to bed, I found myself wrestling with the obvious request my husband had made. Just as I willed myself to be available to my husband, I heard the small voice of a two-year-old echo down the hallway. "Moooommy!" I left my weary husband to take care of my needy child. After settling Evan back to sleep, I tumbled back in bed to my waiting husband. All I wanted was to go to sleep, not meet one more person's needs.

The warmth of the cabin seemed to speak "Welcome" to us as we returned from our walk in the crisp autumn air. The crunch of the leaves under our feet brought back memories of the day we spent at Monroe Reservoir in southern Indiana when we were first dating. As we walked, we reminisced about our first kiss, and we dreamed about what we would do after our children left home.

We had made arrangements for our four children, sixteen-year-old Anne, fourteen-year-old Evan, eleven-year-old Erica, and four-year-old Austin, to spend some time at Grandmother and Granddad's house so we could have a couple of days to get away by ourselves. Earlier in the day, Mark had asked that we go shopping for some new bedroom attire. I hassled him about the request, but secretly looked forward to adding some spice to our love life. After spending some time at the mall shopping for just the right outfit for each of us, we returned to the cabin, took a walk, and began to prepare dinner. We talked, laughed, and enjoyed some playful banter. The cabin, decorated with antiques, featured an old pool table where Mark and I spent the next two hours playing pool, a game we had never played together in our eighteen years of marriage.

I began to anticipate the remainder of our evening and eventually the pleasure of the day together melted into the pleasure of lovemaking.

This wasn't unusual, however. Only days earlier, I had anticipated some lovemaking by dropping hints to my unsuspecting husband all day. I had called him and left a teasing voice mail on his cell phone. Carefully choosing my clothing that day, I selected an outfit Mark had told me drove him crazy. After the kids arrived home from school, I reminded them that tonight was an early-to-bed night to give Mom and Dad some alone time.

After dinner, I pulled Mark aside and kissed him invitingly. We teased one another privately all evening as we helped the kids with their homework, assisted Anne with college applications, took Erica and Evan to piano lessons, gave Austin a bath, and eventually kissed each child goodnight.

I snuggled next to Mark on the couch and welcomed a much-needed back rub. He picked up a book he was reading and shared with me some "you just have to read this" sections. I picked up a pair of Erica's pants that I had begun to hem earlier in the day. I finished the mending project as he read. We enjoyed each other's presence and yet pursued our individual interests, still anticipating the physical intimacy promised earlier in the day. Eventually the playful banter led way to the romance the evening promised. I know without a doubt ... I am a mother *and* a lover.

It is hard to believe that the above scenarios took place within the same marriage. The contrast amazes me. I know that God, in his infinite wisdom, planned for a husband and wife to grow together in oneness. We are to blend our individual lives as we embark upon the journey of marriage. In the early years of marriage, Mark and I found that there were many issues that divided us: both sexual and nonsexual issues. We struggled to make sense of what seemed to be constant conflict.

Our physical relationship was always a source of struggle. His desire was sky high; my desire seemed non-existent. Add to that the demands of children, and we were feeling completely hopeless in making this marriage-thing work.

Eventually, we found ourselves immersed in marriage counseling. We dealt with the issues that were separating us. We talked. We cried. We sorted. We struggled. We learned that neither one of us really understood God's design for marriage or the sexual relationship. We began to go to school, in a sense. We took advantage of resources available to us and started to clear out the misinformation we had come to believe through the years and replaced it with God's truth about marriage and sex. It was a long trip, but a journey worth taking.

Have you ever considered *why* God created sex? Did you know that he finds it beautiful and pleasing that a married man and woman would experience this ultimate level of intimacy? Do you know that God designed us to enjoy our sexuality and to be comfortable with our nakedness within the marriage relationship?

I didn't! Oh sure, I had heard some of those things before, but I hadn't really believed them. I had let my experiences, my lack of knowledge, and my circumstances steal the joy within my marriage.

Is there really sex after kids? My prayer is that this book will answer that question over and over again: Yes, there is! We are going to look at this subject by dividing it into three parts: the plan, the problems, and the practical tools. We'll specifically look at the sexual relationship during the child-rearing years. These are challenging years for a marriage because parenting responsibilities can, and often do, crowd out the time and energy it takes to invest in the marital relationship.

Let's start at the beginning and look back at God's creation of Adam and Eve to understand God's plan for the sexual relationship in marriage. As always, God had a purpose in mind.

God Created Sex!

After God created the beautiful world we live in, he created us. He took the dust of the earth, blew the breath of life into his nostrils, and made man a living being (Genesis 2:7). God then stated, "It is not good for the man to be alone. I will make a helper suitable for him" (2:18). God knew that man could not fully realize his humanity without companionship and a partner in reproduction.

After causing Adam to fall into a deep sleep, God took one of his ribs and made a woman (2:21–22). In describing marriage, God explained that a man is to leave his father and mother and be united to his wife; they will become one flesh (2:24). God finished this creation masterpiece with these words: "The man and his wife were both naked, and they felt no shame" (2:25).

Wow! What powerful words! God's plan for a husband and wife included the ultimate intimacy of vulnerability. He designed nakedness to be a part of marriage.

Two books of the Bible are most helpful in giving us an understanding of the marital relationship and God's design for sex: Genesis and the Song of Solomon. God's Word is not boring or irrelevant to our lives today. On the contrary, he speaks right to our questions and our needs through his truth. He gives boundaries to protect us and freedoms for us to explore and enjoy.

In my journey to understand God's plan for the sexual relationship in marriage, I found that God has three primary reasons for creating the sexual relationship: human reproduction; intimacy; and satisfaction, enjoyment, and pleasure.

Let's take a look at each one of these to understand God's initial design.

The Gift of Life

In Genesis 1:27–28 we read, "So God created man in his own image, in the image of God he created him; male and female he created them. God blessed them and said to them, 'Be fruitful and increase in number; fill the earth and subdue it.'" God was certainly giving the thumbs-up to human reproduction! He was saying, "Expand your families, enjoy the earth, and enjoy the world and the relationships I'm giving you!"

In the first ten years of marriage, our most dysfunctional sexual years, we managed to conceive three babies. According to our ten-year-old daughter, that means we had sex just three times. If you asked Mark about those years, he would agree with her! In truth, it wasn't quite that extreme; I did not struggle with our sexual relationship as long as our goal was to make a baby. However, once we conceived or found ourselves in a season of life where we were not looking to increase our family size, I had little use for our sexual relationship.

I understood only one little piece of God's plan for the sexual relationship and was missing the rest of the pie! My experience is not isolated. I talk to moms all over the world who have a limited view of the sexual relationship in marriage. Do you have a narrow concept of why sex is a part of the marital relationship?

God certainly created the sexual relationship for the purpose of reproduction. But that's not all … there is so much more!

The Gift of Intimacy

God knew that it wasn't good for man to be alone; after all, God created us to be in relationships. He created us with a vertical relationship in mind—our friendship with God—and with a horizontal relationship in mind—our relationship with the people around us. God designed marriage to be the closest human relationship we would experience here on earth.

"Into Me See" (intimacy) is one of the easiest definitions I have ever come across to explain what it means to be intimate. Intimacy allows us to "see" into the life of another. It deepens our human experience. It allows us to feel more fully, trust more deeply, and love more expressively. Intimacy begins with a nonsexual relationship. It finds its roots with conversation, trust, and vulnerability.

Mark and I met on a blind date just two months after I graduated from high school. He was four years older than I and had been living on his own for some time. While we were dating, we could spend hours talking. We talked about our disappointments, our struggles, and even our fears. We shared our hopes, our dreams, and our goals. Just four months after we met, during my freshman year in college, we decided to commit to one another and make this a lifelong partnership. I was nineteen and Mark was twenty-three when we married six months later.

As we talked with each other during our short season of dating, we deepened our intimacy. When we were vulnerable with each other, we were experiencing a "nakedness" of sort. Genesis 2:25, "The man and his wife were both naked, and they felt no shame," may make us think only of physical nakedness, but there is also emotional nakedness to consider. When that level of emotional nakedness is rooted in trust, God's plan includes the ultimate experience of physical intimacy in marriage.

> *"Into Me See" is sharing our deepest thoughts, struggles, and dreams by experiencing an emotional nakedness that brings us one step closer to physical nakedness.*

When a husband and wife experience the sometimes difficult moments of honesty and vulnerability, they build trust and deepen intimacy. "Into Me See" is sharing our deepest thoughts, struggles, and dreams by experiencing an emotional nakedness that brings us one step closer to physical nakedness.

The biblical book of Song of Solomon expressively communicates God's plan for the intimacy shared in marriage. "This is my lover, this is my friend" (5:16). The ultimate intimacy in marriage is knowing your spouse as your best friend. That is when "Into Me See" is fully experienced.

The old King James Version has a great word for intercourse, evident in Genesis 4:1: "And Adam knew Eve his wife; and she conceived." The marital sexual experience is the pinnacle of an intimate personal relationship between husband and wife.

My friend Karen tells me that her husband has always called sex "horizontal fellowship." It has even become a pet phrase they're comfortable using in front of their children. (I can't wait to hear the story from Karen the day one of her kids finally figures out what they are really talking about!) I love that term because it describes the "intimacy piece" of God's plan for marriage. *Fellowship* is defined by Webster's as "companionship; a mutual sharing." God wants us to know the companion with whom we are sharing our life.

God created the sexual relationship for reproduction and intimacy, but that's still not all.

The Gift of Pleasure

As Mark and I worked to understand the gift of sex in our marriage, we discovered a small, yet powerful, book of the Bible: Song of Solomon, sometimes called Song of Songs. This is a beautiful book of poetry and prose describing the love relationship between a man and his wife. It speaks openly of their relationship of love, trust, exclusiveness, spontaneity, and power. It affirms the preciousness of the marriage relationship and emphasizes that it is a gift from God. This book beautifully illustrates that God intends that such love—often grossly distorted and abused by both ancient and modern cultures—be a normal part of marital life in his good creation.[1]

As I began to glimpse the bigger picture of this marital gift, God showed me that there was still more to understanding his plan for sex. As Song of Solomon illustrates, God created the sexual relationship for satisfaction, enjoyment, and pleasure.

In short, he created it for a husband and wife to play together! He created it as a form of recreation. He created it as a beautiful playground just waiting to be explored within the marital relationship.

As we consider a few verses in Song of Solomon, I want you to understand the cast of characters in this book. There are two primary voices in the biblical book of Song of Solomon: the lover and the beloved. The *lover* gives the male perspective and the *beloved* the female perspective.

In the first chapter the lover woos his bride with these words, "How beautiful you are, my darling! Oh, how beautiful! Your eyes are doves."

She then responds with "How handsome you are, my lover! Oh, how charming! And our bed is verdant." When I first read this, I had to look up the word *verdant;* it's not exactly a word I use on a regular basis. It means immature or inexperienced. I love that God sets this forth right at the beginning of the book; he wants us to understand that the sexual relationship is an experience of growing together. It is an opportunity to mature and explore together. God knew that we would need to be reassured that it is okay not to know it all right from the start.

> *God knew that we would need to be reassured that it is okay not to know it all right from the start.*

The conversation about their love relationship continues throughout the book. In chapter 7:6–9 the lover says,

> How beautiful you are and how pleasing, O love, with your delights! Your stature is like that of the palm and your breasts like clusters of fruit. I said, "I will climb the palm tree; I will take hold of its fruit." May your breasts be like the cluster of the vine, the fragrance of your breath like apples, and your mouth like the best wine.

This really gives us a lot to talk about! I told you this was an interesting book to read! God shows us the beauty of expressing physical love. He unabashedly talks about our bodies in their nakedness. He talks about giving and receiving physical pleasure. He creates an environment of sensuality. He even talks about the beauty and the simplicity of kissing when he likens kisses to good wine.

Let's look further at what we find about the physical relationship in Song of Solomon:

- My lover is mine and I am his; he browses among the lilies. (2:16)
- You are a garden fountain, a well of flowing water. (4:15)
- Let my lover come into his garden and taste its choice fruits. (4:16b)
- I am my lover's and my lover is mine. (6:3)
- His left arm is under my head and his right arm embraces me. (8:3)
- I have become ... like one bringing contentment. (8:10)

I love how the Bible often uses the analogy of nature to describe sexual intimacy. Sometimes we see a garden analogy; another time it is water or a flowing stream; often the analogy is of fruit. All of these metaphors for sexual intimacy describe an environment of refreshment. A garden is a place of sensual, fragrant delights. A flowing stream is fresh, cool, sparkling water. Fruit is a sweet, refreshing taste experience.

Here is another selection from the Bible that addresses a husband:

Drink water from your own cistern, running water from your own well. Should your springs overflow in the streets, your streams of water in the public squares? Let them be yours alone, never to be shared with strangers. May your fountain be blessed and may you rejoice in the wife of your youth. A loving doe, a graceful deer—may her

breast satisfy you always, may you ever be captivated by her love (Proverbs 5:15–19).

Dr. Douglas Rosenau paraphrases that verse for wives:
"Rejoice in the husband of your youth. A gentle stag, a
strong deer—may his hand and mouth satisfy you
always, may you ever be captivated by his love."[2]

God has a plan for the marital relationship to be exclu-
sive. He has designed us to be fully intimate with only one
person—the man we married. In Solomon's times, wells
and cisterns were privately owned and very valuable.
What a metaphor for the value of the marital relationship!
Water refreshes us. Drinking from one's own cistern
(one's marital relationship) refreshes a thirsty soul.

Do you see how God values marriage and designed it
for satisfaction? Are you beginning to catch the vision
for a playful sense of recreation and
pleasure God wants us to experience
in marriage?

> *God has a lot to say about sex. He not only wants us to arrive at our destination (growing intimacy), but he wants us to take the scenic routes along the way (satisfaction, enjoyment, and pleasure).*

Entire books have been written
about the Song of Solomon, and I
encourage you to pull out a Bible and
read the entire book yourself. (It's not
very long—usually only six or seven
pages, depending on the version you
have.) If you don't have much experience reading the Bible, I encourage
you to find a version that is easy to
understand and perhaps includes expla-
nations at the bottom of the page. The
NIV Study Bible and the Life Application Bible (NIV)
are both good versions to start with. God has a lot to say
about sex. He not only wants us to arrive at our destination (growing intimacy), but he wants us to take the
scenic routes along the way (satisfaction, enjoyment, and
pleasure).

Yes, there is more to marriage and sex than procreation. The intimacy and delight we have with our spouse is a mirror of the friendship and delight we have with God. And having that intimate relationship with God makes a critical difference in a marriage. Let's look at God's plan for our relationship with him.

The Marriage Triangle

God never designed for us to do marriage alone. Certainly marriage takes two, but in reality it takes three: the husband, the wife, and God. God desires a friendship with us. He's not looking for a relationship that is thought about once a week on Sunday mornings, but rather a life that is lived in relationship with him.

When God created us, he designed us to enjoy a relationship with him. However, God is not one to force his way upon us—he wants us to choose a friendship with him. When we spend time with friends, we often pick up their habits, their phrases, and even their actions.

When we spend time with God, we experience the same thing. God's incredible, unconditional love for us sets the example for marriage. His desire to forgive and extend grace when we mess up models the response we are to extend when our spouse makes a mistake. The intimate relationship with God serves as a first-hand experience of the way we are to treat those we love. As we spend time talking with him and reading his word (the Bible) we begin to pick up his perspectives, his wisdom, and his way of living life. God's ways are always life-giving and marriage-building. When we live like Jesus lived on this earth—handling life with grace and truth—we are on our way to experiencing life the way God created it to be experienced. That's one of the benefits of a friendship with God!

The marital journey is one of intimacy, friendship, exploration, cooperation, pleasure, and joy. It is also an expedition filled with risks, trust, conflict, and sacrifice. God never intended us to make the trip without a map and a Guide. We have already seen portions of the map God has provided: it's his Word, the Bible. And God himself is the only reputable travel Guide for this marital journey. There is no better Guide than the one who made the map! However, God gives us free choice when it comes to choosing him. Many of us travel this journey with a default travel guide: the culture we live in and the world around us. It may seem like the simpler route, but in reality it is full of detours and dead ends along the way and never leads to the destination we desire.

When we say yes to God, when we acknowledge him as the one who will steer us clear of potholes, downed trees, and flooded roadways, we experience faith. He knows how to use a compass, and he is a specialist in finding true north. Faith is trusting in what you cannot see yet believe to be true and trusting the one who knows the journey better than you do. Do you trust God to see the big picture of your life and marriage? Do you believe that he blazed this trail and is the only one who knows the way?

God doesn't promise us there won't be flat tires along the way, but he promises us that he knows how to fix them. When we follow his plans for marriage, we are admitting that he knows the map, created the travel plan, and has our best interest in mind.

Have you trusted God to be your travel guide? If you have never said yes to God, he is waiting for you to invite him on your journey. He's ready to show you the sights along the way—if you let him. I'm not talking about sightseeing trips to church every Sunday, but rather a real journey of truth, faith, and trust. This is about truly knowing him, not just knowing about him. This is not about religion, but a relationship with God.

God does his best work when both husband and wife recognize him as their travel guide. However, there is still great hope even when only one spouse believes. Do you understand that he loved you and me enough to send his son to die for us? Have you accepted him as your Savior and asked him to guide you through your marital journey? If not, I ask you to consider doing that now, before you go any further. Simply pray this prayer:

> *God, I don't want to do this journey alone. I want you to lead. I want to trust that you know the way. Please forgive me for trying to do it on my own. Thank you for sending your son to live on this earth and die on the cross so I could have a personal relationship with you. I accept you as my Savior and Lord.*

With God as your guide, you no longer have to travel this journey alone. No more guessing which way to go and what route to take. Forgiveness and grace abound when you travel with God.

Marriage takes three—that's the way it was designed to be!

The Gift of Sex

God created the sexual relationship in marriage. He created it for human reproduction, for intimacy, and for pure enjoyment and pleasure. He not only desires for us to make love, but to give love back and forth to each other as we enjoy the beauty of the one gift given at the wedding that doesn't need to be wrapped with paper and ribbon. The sexual relationship is a gift from God with a multidimensional purpose.

Have you enjoyed the gift of sex? Are you enjoying all of the facets of this gift? Now that we understand why sex is important, the remainder of this book will focus on how to make it happen in the midst of the child-rearing season of life.

In this chapter, we have looked at God's perfect plan for the sexual relationship. Unfortunately, what God creates for good, humans distort and abuse. Many of us do not experience the fullness of God's plan because of the challenges of our culture, our experiences, our past, or even our season of life. Let's take a look at the challenges we face in experiencing God's plan to the fullest and what we can do to move beyond them.

Personal Reflections

1. RATE the intimacy level of your marriage from 1 to 10, with 10 being deep intimacy and 1 being no intimacy.

2. IDENTIFY one of God's truths you learned in this chapter that can take your marriage a step higher on the intimacy scale.

3. READ Song of Solomon one day this week. If your husband is willing, read it together with him.

For Husbands Only

The chapter your wife just read was designed to help you understand God's plan for the sexual relationship in marriage. Much of what I learned about sex came from the locker room, the streets, and even pornography. When Jill and I encountered problems in our marriage, and specifically in our sexual relationship, I began to realize how much information I had that was just plain wrong.

I had a lot to learn about loving and serving my wife. I had a skewed version of what my wife desired sexually and had to learn what real women want rather than the garbage I learned from magazines. I had to learn what true intimacy really was.

There is a book of the Bible known as Song of Solomon. It is an entire book of the Bible about sex! It's about loving and desiring each other in marriage. It's about understanding God's design for satisfaction, enjoyment, and pleasure. Your wife might ask you to read it with her. (It's only six or seven pages. Don't get overwhelmed!) Consider reading it together. The benefits may surprise you both!

Mark

part 2

The Problems—
Issues Affecting
Sexual Intimacy

chapter 2

Intimacy Inhibitors

ONE CHRISTMAS, unbeknownst to the other, Mark's parents and my parents both decided to give us a complete set of luggage. We walked away from our holiday gatherings with eight new suitcases in a variety of shapes and sizes! Neither set of parents knew the other had chosen to give the same gift! When we opened the second set of luggage, we teasingly asked if there was a conspiracy to send us somewhere. Mark asked which suitcase contained the tickets to Hawaii.

There were no tickets to Hawaii that Christmas. Our extended family simply knew that we needed new luggage. We had both brought old suitcases into our marriage and had never invested in new luggage. As we added more children to our family, we would just stuff the suitcases with more clothes.

When Mark and I married we blended our lives, our dreams, and our belongings. We also both brought our own "baggage" into the marriage relationship. And I'm not just talking about suitcases. I'm referring to the baggage we carry from our childhood experiences, the misconceptions and misperceptions about relationships, along with our hurts, struggles, shame, and doubt. We brought our mistakes from the past and tried to turn them into hopes for the future. Some of those suitcases we tried to hide away, hoping that no one would ever find them. Some of them we identified but left closed, fearing too much information might damage this newly created family.

Everybody brings baggage into the marital relationship. Conflict resolution, trust, friendship experiences, religious upbringing ... all of these are differences we bring into our new family. Some of those suitcases are filled with experiences and misconceptions about the sexual relationship. These often erroneously define who we are sexually. Sometimes they hinder us from fully enjoying God's gift of sex.

If we are going to experience completely God's design for marriage, we have to be willing to open up some of those suitcases. We have to be willing to find the areas of our lives where we have entertained lies and replace them with truth ... God's truth. We have to identify misconceptions we have believed and make choices today that will not cause damage to the marriage relationship in the future.

Are you ready to do a little bit of exploring? Let's open some of the suitcases we might have carried into our marriage.

Common Challenges

Common challenges are baggage that many of us carry and need to understand.

Suitcase #1: Media

Our media-saturated culture plays a huge role in our thoughts about sex. As one mom put it, "If you believed everything you watched on TV and at the movie theatre, you'd be questioning yourself all the time. Personally, I don't know of any worn-out, exhausted mom whose sexuality button is turned on with one kiss—yet, that's what you see in the movies."

What we watch and read does become part of who we are and what we think. Consider the potential impact today's media can have on us.

Movies

What is most dangerous about movies? The comparison game we play in our minds. Although we don't realize it, we often compare our very *real* life to a very *unreal* situation on the big screen.

The first place we start is with our appearance. For instance, you're watching a movie with a sexually intimate scene. Without realizing it, you say to yourself, "Wow. If my husband looked like Tom Cruise, it could be that way for us." Or maybe you compare yourself to the screen, thinking, "You know, if I only looked like Nicole Kidman, our sex life could be better." The problem with this is that neither Tom Cruise nor Nicole Kidman looks that way in real life. (Nor do they act that way in real life, as they are now divorced—so much for the perfect couple, huh?) Today's movie producers have a wide variety of tools available to them to enhance what we see. A soft-focus filter, makeup, and computer editing can go a long way in creating the perfect, smooth-skinned body we often see on the screen.

How about some more unrealistic comparisons? I don't know about you, but I've never had a full orchestra in my bedroom. But isn't that what happens in the movies? The music swells at just the right time. The lighting is perfect. And when it's all said and done, we have never seen anyone have to clean up after sex on the Hollywood screen! How real is that?

It's not real! It's not real at all. We have to grasp hold of this now before any more damage is done! When we play the comparison game, we are setting ourselves up for discontentment. Each time we say, "Wow, my life is not like that," or entertain the thought, "I wish my life was like that," we become just a little bit more discontent with our circumstances. Then we become discontented with our spouses, because they don't measure up to what we have just seen in the movies. It is a very dangerous game to play.

Movies also idealize relationships outside of marriage. They have a way of making us justify sin by causing us to become a champion for the underdog even if immorality is present. They also rarely show the consequences of sex outside of marriage, carefully selecting what we watch on the screen and leaving out the real details that would otherwise ruin a "perfect story."

> Each time we say, "Wow, my life is not like that," or entertain the thought, "Wow, I wish my life was like that," we become just a little bit more discontent with our circumstances. Then we become discontented with our spouses, because they don't measure up to what we have just seen in the movies. It is a very dangerous game to play.

I remember watching *The Bridges of Madison County* and feeling sorry for the character played by Meryl Streep. Her inattentive husband was unavailable, and her children were wrapped up in their own lives. When she found "love" from the stranger who happened by while her family was away at the fair, I mentally began to justify the relationship. That's when I caught myself and realized how this movie was softening my view of sex outside of marriage. Hollywood does indeed make a profound impact on our thinking.

Magazines

Most secular magazines come from a "disposable-marriage" and "affairs-are-a-normal-way-of-life" mindset. A regular diet of these magazines will lead us to think that if marriage is too hard—just get out. Forgiveness, commitment, and sacrificial love are not found on the pages of our culture's most popular women's magazines.

Novels

Many of the romance novels on the bookshelves are simply R-rated movies in book form. In the same way that movies paint an unreal picture of life, romance novels open the door to the comparison game. The story, complete with the hero and heroine, is setting us up for disappointment when we compare this not-real story to our very real lives. We have to choose our reading material wisely.

Television

When I first began staying home with our daughter, I began watching a soap opera every day. I never gave thought to the subtle messages to which I was exposing my mind. Affairs, complicated relationships, and poor communication skills are commonplace on television dramas. Romance and skewed conflict resolution all come to some sense of completeness at the end of thirty minutes in a sitcom. Once again, *it's not real!* We have to understand that, or else we'll drive ourselves crazy trying to measure up to a standard that is impossible to meet.

Ways to Unpack

So how do we live in a media-saturated culture and not be affected by it? Unless you want to live in a cave and have no contact with the outside world, I don't believe there is any way to be completely unaffected by the media. However, there are ways we can be *less* affected by it. Here are some suggestions:

- Learn to discern. Just because a movie is at the theater or on the video store shelf, it doesn't mean we need to see it. Make a commitment not to view sexually explicit movies, which would include most R-rated movies. Use a resource such as www.pluggedinmag.com to evaluate movies you are thinking about watching.

- Choose your reading material wisely. When sitting in a waiting room surrounded by magazines, stop and consider what you are about to feed your mind.
- Determine ahead of time what you will and will not watch, rather than simply hitting the clicker on the TV remote and surfing channels.
- Limit movie and TV viewing to shows that do not idealize sex outside of marriage. If soap operas have captured your time, choose another form of entertainment in the afternoon.
- Be willing to turn off movies and television shows if you discover they are sexual junk food.
- Choose to read inspirational fiction rather than secular fiction. Look for books published by Zondervan, Bethany House, Moody, and other Christian publishers whose books are based upon the principles of courage, commitment, and integrity.
- Read magazines that will encourage you in marriage and God-honoring sexuality. Christianity Today, Inc. produces *Today's Christian Woman* and *Marriage Partnership*—excellent magazines that encourage you to live the way God designed.

Our bodies need nutritious, wholesome food. Too much junk food can affect our weight, our skin, and our ability to fight illness. Similarly our minds need wholesome nutrition. Media junk food affects our attitudes, our choices, and our ability to discern between right and wrong. That's why God says, "Whatever is true, whatever is noble, whatever is right, whatever is pure, whatever is lovely, whatever is admirable—if anything is excellent or praiseworthy—think about such things" (Philippians 4:8–9).

God knew that we would have many choices when it came to the things of this world. He knew we would struggle to make good decisions—that's why he even went as far as to tell us what to feed our minds. Are you bringing media baggage into your marriage? Toss out some of those suitcases now!

Suitcase #2: Slang Terminology

Not only does our culture openly discuss sex outside of marriage, it also attaches slang terminology to destructively distort God's gift of sexuality. These inappropriate words cheapen the sexual relationship and seep into our subconscious thinking about sex.

You and I need to identify the terms we've heard over the years and consider the destructive connotation they imply. Even the simple phrase "talking dirty," when someone describes a person talking about sex, implies that sex is dirty. Do you see how that affects our thinking?

As married women, we need to use correct biological terms for parts of the human body. If you've never openly discussed sex, you may find yourself uncomfortable with any sexual terms. Practice saying them aloud when you are alone to become more comfortable talking about sex. Then choose respectful, correct terms, rather than cultural slang when talking with your spouse about sex.

Is it appropriate that you and your husband have pet names or a secret vocabulary you share when talking about sex? Absolutely. Many couples have special words or phrases they use in private. This deepens the bond of intimacy in your relationship. However, the purpose of this is to enhance the loving, exciting process of making love. Rosenau was right when he said, "If any language is demeaning, offensive, harmfully aggressive, or cheap to either mate, it should be avoided."[3]

Suitcase #3: Parental Instruction about Sex

Mark and I often refer to the homes in which we grew up as our home internship experiences. It is where we witnessed healthy or unhealthy conflict resolution. Our sense of right and wrong was established or tainted here. And, for good or bad, the home in which you grew up set the foundation for your sex education.

Like me, you probably had sex ed in health class in junior high and high school, where you learned facts about the human body and reproduction. But what you will take into your adulthood is not as much *facts* as *attitude.* Your attitude about your sexuality was most likely set in the framework of the family in which you were raised. Some of us were raised with a healthy understanding of sexuality. We saw a loving, even playful relationship in our parents' marriage. We understood that God created sex to be beautiful when experienced within the protection of the marital relationship. Yet many of us probably carried some baggage into our marriage because we experienced negative attitudes.

"We Don't Talk About That in This House."

When things can't be discussed, we associate them with being bad. If we have to whisper about it and talk about it behind closed doors, it must be something forbidden. If this was the mind-set you were raised with, you may well associate sex as being something shameful and even disgusting. You might not really understand the beautiful gift God has given you. It is possible you do not fully enjoy your own sexuality.

"You *Don't* Have Sex Before You Get Married."

This message focuses on the *don't* more than the *do* of sex. It associates sex with a negative connotation rather than a positive implication, leaving out the beautiful gift that God has given to a husband and wife. Baggage from this message might include being uncomfortable with the whole sexual part of the marriage because "don't, don't, don't" has been so ingrained in the mind.

"Sex Is Something You Endure, Dear."

Well-meaning but ill-informed grandmothers and mothers have often passed on negative connotations about marital sex. The concept that sex is for men to enjoy and women to endure denies God's beautiful plan for physical intimacy. This kind of false information plants the seeds of inhibition and shame.

"Sex Is Okay Before Marriage As Long As You Are Responsible."

Some parents, who came from the "free sex" generation themselves, may have even encouraged sexual experimentation. In this home, birth control might have even been encouraged or provided by the parent. If you were raised in this kind of environment, you were probably greatly influenced by what you saw or read in the media or what you heard in the locker room at school. This experience often places unrealistic expectations on marriage because the media misinformation has presented an unreal picture of love and relationship and the sexual experiences have come without a long-term, monogamous commitment. Locker room talk and the pursuance of "free sex" is always about sex rather than love, and gives a skewed experience of the physical relationship. It also lacks any concept of a marital commitment being a requirement for good sex.

Ways to Unpack

In each of these cases, a lack of information or misinformation leads to inhibition and confusion. If you can relate to any of these, consider doing a new internship to learn about God's beautiful plan for physical relationship in marriage. Start by rereading Song of Solomon in your Bible. I also suggest Tommy Nelson's book *The Book of Romance*, which will help you gain an in-depth understanding of Song of Solomon and further expand your mind to God's beautiful design for physical intimacy in marriage.

Suitcase #4—Previous Relationships

What's the Problem?

Today's mothers are the product of the sexual revolution that began in the 1960s and continues today. According to our culture, sex is not reserved for marriage; it's a healthy part of any relationship. Because we are so influenced by the cries of culture, many of us entered marriage with one or more suitcases labeled "previous sexual relationship."

You may have carried previous-relationship baggage into your marriage even if you never had premarital intercourse. Those suitcases might be labeled mistrust, fear, jealousy, shame, or anger. They represent a filter through which we process our marriage. Whether we realize it or not, previous relationships do affect our marriage. We are a sum of our experiences, so it becomes difficult to separate ourselves from what we have known.

Tonya had been married five years. She and her husband, Ted, asked Mark and me to mentor them as their marriage was hurting. We met weekly for several months, helping them open their suitcases one by one. One piece of her baggage was from a previous relationship.

For several years Tonya had lived with a critical, controlling man whose demeaning words caused emotional injury. Anytime they were intimate, this man criticized her body. "Your breasts are too small. Your hips are too big. You need to lose a few pounds again." She heard these messages on a regular basis.

Tonya eventually left that relationship. Then she met Ted, a wonderful, loving man who asked her to marry him. Ted loved her as she had never been loved before, yet Tonya couldn't bring herself to allow Ted to see her without clothes. For five years, their intimate moments had to take place with the lights out and under the covers.

If he was in the bathroom while she was showering, she required that he leave the room when she exited the shower. Even though Ted had never criticized her body in any way, Tonya's baggage from the previous relationship was damaging her beautiful marriage. She had been wounded so deeply by the other relationship that she couldn't bring herself to trust anyone to see her body.

That's an example of the damage that previous relationships can bring into a marriage. We compare and create expectations. We live in fear or defensiveness because of our previous experiences.

Both Mark and I were sexually active before we were married. We both brought unrealistic expectations and unfounded fears into our sexual relationship. Personally, I struggled with the "desire" piece of the puzzle. I asked myself, "Why did I have desire before I was married and little or no desire after marriage?" I decided to ask God that question, and over time he showed me that my sexual desire before marriage was built on rebellion, not love. I knew sex outside of marriage was something I wasn't supposed to do, so the desire was heightened as I felt I was partaking of a forbidden fruit. When Mark and I married, suddenly the forbidden fruit was gone.

Brian and Heather Jamison, in their *Marriage Partnership* article "Haunted by Premarital Sex," put it this way: "The familiarity of marriage lessened the lure of what was previously forbidden—sex. Without the illicitness surrounding sex, we began to see our premarital relationship for what it really was—counterfeit intimacy." Many of us carry the suitcase of counterfeit intimacy into our marriages.[4]

Brian and Heather identify the real heart of this issue:

> Due to the downplay of the negative effects of consensual premarital sex by both the secular world and well-meaning Christians, its consequences are often ignored and allowed to wreak havoc in marriages ...

over extended periods of time. As time moves forward, it can be difficult for a couple to dig down to the heart of the problem.

Unfortunately, many of us focus on the symptoms of our problems rather than digging down to the root issues that are often buried deep within our hearts and minds.

If you are in a second marriage, after divorce or widowhood, it is possible that a few emotional suitcases accompanied you into this marriage union. Many churches offer divorce recovery groups to help identify unhealthy baggage that can be carried from one relationship to the next. Contact your local church or check out www.divorce-care.org to find a group near you.

What's the Solution?

What is the process for unpacking previous-relationship suitcases you have carried into your marriage? Here are some steps to opening the suitcase, accepting forgiveness, and moving forward.

1. *Acknowledge.* This happens when we call premarital sex what it is: a sin. It is a rebellion against God. When we truly acknowledge what premarital sex is and stop rationalizing it for whatever reason, we are on our way to finding freedom from the damage it is causing in our marriage. Step 1 concludes with saying to God, "I'm sorry. Will you please forgive me?"

2. *Accept Forgiveness.* God doesn't rank sins. They are all the same in his eyes. When Jesus died on the cross, he took our place for being condemned for our sins. When we accept Jesus as our Savior and live in his love and grace, the door is open to have a relationship with God. When we ask God for forgiveness and then accept his grace and forgiveness, our guilt is wiped away. This is when

we experience true freedom in Christ and begin to find sexual freedom in our marriage. Step 2 ends with thanking God for his forgiveness and grace.

3. *Forgive Yourself.* Once you ask God for forgiveness, he wipes the slate clean. Make a conscious decision to forgive yourself for the poor decisions you made. Bask in God's grace and rejoice in the ability to start over again.

4. *Extend Forgiveness.* If your husband was sexually active before marriage and you have held that against him, choose to forgive. Allow the slate to be wiped clean by extending love and grace to him.

5. *Start a New Internship.* When sex is experienced before marriage, it is often based on lust, instant gratification, and rebellion. Building a marriage on this foundation is like building a house on sand. A strong foundation occurs when the marriage relationship is built on God's plan. This may mean a season of rebuilding by reading God's Word and seeking educational opportunities through marriage counseling, books, seminars, and retreats.

Suitcase #5—Religion

In spite of growing up in a church, I'm not sure I ever remember hearing specific teaching on sex, though I did have an understanding that sex before marriage was wrong. It was not discussed much, but understood in general. I also remember that the voices of my friends and my culture spoke far louder than the quiet teaching of the church.

I believe our churches still have some work to do in communicating the beauty of the marital sexual relationship. Clifford and Joyce Penner agree with this as they share their journey of understanding God's plan for sexuality in their book *The Gift of Sex*. After searching the Bible to understand God's plan for their marriage, they wrote, "We came out convinced that the Bible is a very prosexual book. We had heard our church's message about the "don'ts" of sexual behavior outside marriage, and, lacking a balancing positive input about sex in marriage, had generalized to the point that we thought the church's message entirely negative."[5]

Rosenau furthers this point by stating that some churches teach a legalistic, restrictive sexual environment that robs couples of the ability to enjoy God's intended pleasure. Not too long ago, sex was justified only for the purposes of reproduction in some denominations. In general the Christian community has been unwilling to openly discuss God's beautiful design for the sexual pleasure in marriage. At the very least, the approach has been unbalanced.[6]

Evaluate the teaching (or lack of teaching) you have received from your religious experience. Has it been balanced in representing the boundary of no sex before marriage as well as the beauty of sex within marriage? If not, keep your student hat on; you and I have a lot to learn about God's plan for the sexual relationship in marriage.

Suitcase #6—Poor Conflict-Resolution Skills

Do you sulk when your husband doesn't pay attention to you? Do you express anger by slamming cabinet doors or stomping through the house? Are your words or tone cutting or demeaning? Do you say everything is okay when really it isn't? Do you withhold sex or affection in order to "punish" your spouse? Do you have trouble saying, "I'm sorry; will you please forgive me"? If you answered yes to any of the above questions, you most likely carried a suitcase into your marriage filled with unhealthy conflict resolution skills.

In marriage there will be conflict. Two human beings cannot live life together and not have conflict; it will happen. That given, it is important to understand how to handle conflict when we're faced with it. If we short-circuit conflict resolution, we will find the concept of giving and receiving sexual love very difficult.

First, we have to understand that conflict, if handled appropriately, can strengthen our marriage relationship. We must learn to listen and reflect back to each other what the other is saying rather than defending ourselves against inaccuracies. We need to listen in order to "hear" his feelings, rather than analyze whether his feelings are right or wrong. We have to help our partner feel valued, loved, and secure even in the midst of conflict.

Second, we need to focus on resolution rather than winning. If one of us is focused on the goal of winning the argument, conflict cannot be resolved. Resolution happens when we share and engage each other in conversation with the purpose of reaching an agreement we both can live with.

Third, we have to learn how to bring closure to our conflict. Usually conflict happens because we have both been wrong in one way or another. Often one of us makes an insensitive or wrong choice. Then the other reacts to the infraction, and we find ourselves angry with each other. Closure happens when we "own" our part of the conflict, offer an apology, and ask for forgiveness. When forgiveness is extended by the offended party, the relationship is restored.

Most couples only offer half apologies to each other. Spouses stop at "I'm sorry." (Actually, many of us have trouble even uttering those two words!) However, "I'm sorry" is just the beginning of an apology. "I'm sorry; will you please forgive me?" is a full apology. The closure to the conflict happens when the other person can say, "I forgive you."

Did you carry this suitcase into your marriage? If so, commit to unpack it today!

Major Challenges

Major Challenges are bigger issues that, unfortunately, some of us have to face.

Abortion

Dear Hearts at Home,

Two years ago I attended a workshop at your conference about healing from abortion. I want to let you know what an important part it has played in my healing.

At nineteen, as a freshman in college, I found myself unmarried and pregnant. I made the decision to get an abortion. I walked out of the clinic rid of the "problem," chin held high, and I died on the inside. My secret was covered, tucked away, but life wasn't the same after that. I determined to be "perfect" and hoped maybe God would forgive me if I was really good. I eventually married and became a mother of two.

The next five years found me unhappy as I kept my family at a distance and maintained a very busy schedule so I wouldn't have to think. Anxiety and sleeplessness prevailed, and I rationalized that it was my job, the house we lived in, the kids, my husband, PMS. Everyone else had a problem, not me.

Soon fear and a sense of impending doom set in, and I was terrified something bad was going to happen to me or the kids. Guilt, shame, and fear set in. I knew God said, "Thou shalt not murder," but I had murdered my own child. I thought God was going to reach out of the sky and squash me. Panic attacks began.

Finally, having nowhere else to turn, I turned to God. The very one I was running from, I finally realized, was the only one who could help me heal. As I began the slow healing process through counseling, I attended the Hearts at Home conference and signed up to attend the workshop about healing from abortion. That's when I was introduced to the Healing Hearts ministry, where I learned how to find true freedom from my past. Thank you for connecting me to the One who has given me a new life!

Sincerely,
Darcy

I received the above letter just three days before I wrote this chapter. A coincidence? Absolutely not. A God-cidence, that's what it is.

If abortion is a suitcase you carry from your past, I hope Darcy's letter gives you hope. Most women find that abortion guilt, also known as Post-Abortion Syndrome (PAS), surfaces many years down the road, often after they've become mothers.

If abortion is a part of your past, it is a suitcase that can't be hidden and forgotten. It is often the guilt, shame, and secrecy that keeps women from experiencing beautiful, healthy sexual relationships with their husbands. Most women look everywhere else to figure out what's wrong with their marriages.

God wants you to experience healing. Healing Hearts ministry (www.healinghearts.org) is an organization of integrity that can help you find the healing you desire so deeply.

Sexual Abuse

Mary's life changed when she was five years old and her father began to visit her bedroom at night. The abuse continued until she was old enough to leave home some fifteen years later. When she married, the damaging impact of those years of violation became apparent.

Women who experience sexual abuse often find their reactions to the sexual relationship in marriage in one of two categories: They desire sex greatly (often more than their spouses), or they detest it immensely.

Mary found herself in the first category. Her desire was far greater than her husband's, and she felt rejected by his lack of desire. She equaled sex with love based upon what her father had told her in all those years of abuse. When her husband didn't respond to her advances, she felt unloved.

Entire books have been written about recovering from childhood sexual abuse. I cannot do justice to the topic in a small section of this book. I do, however, want to communicate hope that you can find freedom from the past.

Through counseling, knowing God's truth, and understanding his beautiful plan for our lives, there is healing and hope if you have been the victim of childhood sexual abuse. God can heal. He is hope. Don't let this baggage rob you of your joy any longer. Grab hold of God's promise that indeed he will restore what the locusts have eaten (Joel 2:25).

If you have been a victim of sexual abuse, please know that I am praying for you. I have committed to pray for every woman who reads this book, but I have a special place in my heart for those of you who have carried this baggage into your marriage.

Lies and Truths

Linda Dillow and Lorraine Pintus address healing from sexual abuse in their book *Intimate Issues.* They expose the lie that keeps us from finding healing and the truths that set us free. What is the lie?

Lie: Satan says, "God doesn't care about sexual abuse, and He certainly doesn't care about you. Otherwise He would have intervened and stopped your abuser."

Truth: God says, "I love you. I hate sexual abuse and I am deeply grieved over what your abuser did to you. I will punish your offender, and his punishment will be just. I desire to heal you and set you free."[7]

The question I most often hear about recovering from abuse is "If God loves me, why didn't he stop my abuser?"

This question must be answered to allow you to move forward in your healing. God didn't stop your abuser because, when he created humans, he gave us free will. We have the ability to choose right or wrong. If we didn't have free will, we would operate on this earth like puppets, doing whatever we were told and unable to make decisions for ourselves. Unfortunately, your abuser made a wrong choice, and you were the victim of his sinful actions.

What God wants more than anything is to bring you comfort and healing. Lorraine and Linda go on to break down the truths God wants you to understand:

1. *God loves you.* In Ephesians 3:17–19 we read, "I pray that you ... may ... grasp how wide and long and high and deep is the love of Christ, and to know this love that surpasses knowledge."
2. *God hates sexual abuse.* In the Old Testament, serious sexual crimes were punishable by death. God speaks very clearly about the design for sexual relations within the marriage union only.
3. *Your offender will be punished.* Proverbs 11:21 tells us, "Be sure of this: The wicked will not go unpunished." You may see this in your lifetime or you may not, but you can be assured of God's accountability.
4. *God desires to heal you.* God wants to hold you and comfort you, but unlike your abuser, he will not touch you against your will. He waits for you to turn to him, waits for you to extend your hand and receive the gifts he longs to give.[8]

Steps to Healing

In no way do I want to simplify what is a long process of healing. However, I want to give some direction if you are ready to make the first steps in healing.

1. *Find a Christian counselor you like.* Many people falsely believe they need to stick with the first counselor they find. Interview counselors, visit a few, and then settle on one with whom you feel comfortable. Some women find the expertise of two or three counselors over several years' time has been helpful.

2   *Allow yourself time.* The healing process often takes years and involves sorting through a myriad of emotions and lies from the enemy. Don't be overwhelmed with the length of time; we're talking months or years of investment to secure a lifetime of freedom. It's an investment of time worth taking.

3. *Process what you are learning with your husband, if possible.* This keeps him in the loop of communication and helps him to know where you are emotionally.

4. *Begin relearning about God's plan for relationships and sex.* Read books, attend seminars, read Song of Solomon; do whatever it takes to begin a new internship.

Before I leave this topic, I want to note that even a one-time sexual violation, which you may not consider in the category of abuse, may have a profound effect on your marital relationship. My friend Beth discovered this to be true. As a teenager, Beth had traveled to visit a male friend of hers. Although they were just good friends, one night Beth awoke to find her "friend" in her bed fondling her. She immediately told him to leave the room, and he obliged. Her friendship with this boy fizzled after that point, and Beth never gave much thought to what had happened.

Years later, when her husband became affectionate at night or when Beth was barely awake, she felt intense anger. She couldn't understand why she responded so strongly to this one particular expression of sexual interest. Finally, Beth decided to pray about it and ask God to show her the root of this anger. In an answer to her prayer, God brought back the memory of what had happened that night years before. She had not given any prolonged thought to that moment, but now she realized the impact it had made on her. She shared what she remembered with her husband and found herself finally able to experience some freedom from a past experience.

If the baggage you have carried into your marriage weighs in heavily, like sexual abuse, author Neil Anderson has written several books that are excellent healing resources. *Victory Over the Darkness* and *The Bondage Breaker* are both designed to help people unpack the suitcases they've carried into adulthood. There is hope!

Affairs

Jenny sat across the table from me, tears streaming down her face. She had just discovered that her husband was having an affair. I listened as she poured out her heart, questioning everything about their relationship.

God knew what he was doing when he made "Do not commit adultery" one of the Ten Commandments. Infidelity is devastating to a marriage. Hollywood sensationalizes adultery by luring us to believe it is the way to handle a less-than-ideal marriage. In reality, it damages the very fibers of marriage: trust, communication, and love.

It is not only men who have affairs. In the past year, Mark and I have mentored three couples that were rebuilding relationships after the wives had had affairs.

Can marriage survive the damage of an affair? Yes, it can. With God's grace and forgiveness there is indeed hope in surviving and even thriving after an affair. Here's what we have learned while helping dozens of couples survive and recover from an affair:

1. *Get help!* Locate a Christian counselor and commit to getting the help needed to find healing. Yes, it may cost some money and it's indeed an investment of time, but it is time and money well spent. Your marriage is worth fighting for.
2. *Allow time for grieving and healing.* It usually takes at least a year to rebuild broken trust. That's if both parties are cooperative and ready to make this work. It's not impossible, but it takes a season of healing.
3. *Allow one another to experience emotional highs and lows.* The recovery phase is a heart-wrenching time of sorting through feelings. Denial, anger, and emotional exhaustion are all emotions of the healing process.
4. *Reinstate full honesty into the marriage.* Refrain from too many detail questions about the affair, but explore questions that help process the marriage relationship, such as How did we get here? What needs to change? What can be done to rebuild trust?
5. *Understand the process of forgiveness.* Forgiveness is essential in the healing process. Forgiveness is a choice we make to bring about healing. However, we don't forgive and forget. Forgiveness puts you on a healing path but does not condone what has been done. Nor does it reinstate trust; that is earned slowly over time.

Dr. Douglas Rosenau addresses healing from adultery in his book *A Celebration of Sex:*

The cheater wonders if [the questions] will ever stop and trust will ever be rebuilt. This is part of the penance and price paid to restore intimacy and heal the damage done. An adulterer has stolen intimacy and commitment from the partner. Restitution in kind seems appropriate, not only to heal what has been damaged, but also to help that person grow through penitence and make some real changes. Time, money, and energy should be invested in rebuilding the marital intimacy that has been so damaged by the adultery.[9]

Dr. Rosenau goes on to say, "If both partners are committed to restoring the marriage, they almost always succeed. The trauma often creates a deeper and more realistic intimacy with better boundaries in place. Greater maturity grows out of the crisis they have weathered."

Is there hope for a marriage that experiences adultery? Absolutely.

Pornography and Sexual Addiction

Mark and I sat in the counselor's office discussing our damaged marriage and our dysfunctional sex life. We had been seeing the counselor for several months and had successfully worked through many of our communication and conflict resolution struggles. We were starting to put new tools to use in our daily relationship, allowing us to experience a new level of trust in each other. Nevertheless, our sexual relationship was in the worst shape it had ever been. That's when we realized the damage pornography continued to bring to our marriage.

Mark remembers seeing pornography as a grade-schooler. It was readily available to him in a variety of places. As a teenager and young adult, Mark felt pornography was a regular part of any real man's reading material.

When Mark was twenty-two years old, he made a decision to accept Jesus Christ as his personal Savior at a Billy Graham crusade. Slowly he changed his lifestyle to embrace his newfound faith. Eventually, the pornography disgusted him and he looked at it for the last time.

Shortly thereafter Mark and I met and married. Our first year was wedded bliss, but after we started our family during our second year of marriage, the struggles set in. Seven years later we sat in a marriage counselor's office trying to understand what had gone wrong. When it came to our sexual relationship, we soon learned that the pornography lies were still embedded in Mark's mind. And he hadn't seen it in seven years!

In *The Sexual Man*, Archibald Hart states that his research study indicated that 94 percent of Christian men admitted that they had been exposed to or viewed pornography some time in their life.[10]

What are the lies pornography tells men? Pornographic pictures and articles falsely communicate that women's bodies should look a certain way. They state that women will act a certain way sexually. They inaccurately present women as sexual fanatics, only to set a husband up for disappointment when he finds his wife is not responding like she "should."

What's the damage of pornography? Its lies about sex become ingrained in our minds. Pornography makes sex into a sport and people into sex objects for selfish sexual gratification. It is far from God's design for a sexual union in marriage. When pornography is the standard for sex, it causes discontent in the marital relationship and places unrealistic expectations on the physical relationship.

For Mark, with pornography as the standard, our sexual encounters were never often enough or good enough for him. His off-the-chart expectations never allowed for satisfaction.

For me, I could never trust Mark's touch, as it always seemed sexual in nature. I grew to resent our physical relationship and felt it was something I just had to endure to make him happy once a week.

All of that damage ... and Mark hadn't seen pornography in seven years! Imagine the destruction that happens every day in homes where pornography is viewed regularly.

Several years ago we spent months helping Linda and Larry restore their marriage after pornography had ravaged their relationship. Larry's addiction to internet pornography was out of control. Sneaking on the computer at night and even accessing it at work were evidences of addictive behavior.

As we sat at our kitchen table and discussed the hurt this was causing as well as the damage it was doing to their relationship, Linda said, through her tears, "I feel like I'm sleeping with the hundreds of women he's been looking at." There is a spiritual truth here that Linda experienced. God knows the power of the mind, and because of that Jesus taught, "You have heard that it was said, 'Do not commit adultery.' But I tell you that anyone who looks at a woman lustfully has already committed adultery with her in his heart" (Matthew 5:27–28).

Jennifer and Jeff faced similar challenges in their marriage. Jeff was drawn to X-rated movies that he rented secretly when Jennifer wasn't around. When Jennifer discovered what Jeff was doing, she could not bring herself to make love to her husband. She felt used and was angry at the deception.

Like a siren in Greek mythology who lured sailors to their deaths on rocky coasts with her seductive singing, pornography lures men to their basements, their laptops, and their PCs resulting in emotional death and the death of marital intimacy. The voice that calls them is that of the enemy who whispers the lies of sex without the responsibilities of relationship. It is a dead end street that leads to destruction.

Like the other major challenges we have addressed, there is hope! God has given us a plan for restoration of relationships. Of course, if we all would follow his instruction book—the Bible—we wouldn't have to deal with the consequences of our choices or our spouses' choices. But that only happens in a perfect world, and we don't live in a perfect world.

Just like the other major challenges, there is healing to be found from sexual addiction and pornography. It is not something that goes away on its own. Usually, we need some help sorting through the deep-seated issues and long-term habits that need to be identified. It is a process of renewing the mind and heart.

Mark found that he needed to replace the enemy's lies with God's truth when it came to a healthy sexual relationship. I had my own issues as well that were creating difficulty in our marriage. It was a relearning process for both of us. We found success because we worked hard to renew our minds.

What If He Is Unwilling to Seek Help?

Wouldn't it be great if both husband and wife realized they needed help, sought it out, and found their relationship healed and renewed within a matter of months? That would be wonderful, but unfortunately it is not the way it usually works.

Many times in our healing process, Mark and I would find ourselves at different places of conviction and interest in getting help. I would desire help and he would be ready to give up. Weeks later he was ready to dig in and make changes, and I was feeling like throwing in towel, weary from the difficult relational work. Eventually, we both wanted it enough to get the help needed and make the necessary changes to improve and renew our relationship.

But what if you are the only one who sees the need for help? What if you are the only one who seems to think there is a problem? What do you do? Is there any hope if only one person in the relationship wants to see it improve? The answer is yes, there is hope.

You and I need to make right choices even in the midst of any wrong choices our husbands might make. When one of us makes God-honoring, right choices, it is character building for us. When our character reflects more of Christ, we find a sense of peace even in the midst of a difficult relationship.

Leslie Vernick addresses this in her book *How to Act Right When Your Spouse Acts Wrong.* "As we start learning how to act right when our spouse acts wrong, we will begin to see what God is doing to make us more like him in the midst of marital difficulties."[11]

Leslie goes on to say,

> Acting right when our spouse acts wrong will not necessarily guarantee a more satisfying marital relationship, although it often does. Acting right may not make our spouse turn around and change his or her ways or meet our needs, although it could. God says that we exert a powerful influence over others as we seek to lovingly interact with them.[12]

We need to act right when our spouses act wrong, because it's the right thing to do—not because it might make them change. We need to grow our characters, not manipulate our spouses.

I remember when I was on the receiving end of someone trying to act right for the wrong reasons. As Mark began to meet my needs and help around the house, he did so with the purpose of getting more sex. When he transitioned from doing those things expecting a reward in return, to doing those things because they were serving and loving, I felt valued and loved and our relationship improved.

If your husband will not seek help, but you feel the need to get help, make an appointment for yourself with a counselor or a mentor. Don't wait for your husband to come around; work on your own baggage. Unpack a few of your own suitcases. Take the plank out of your own eye before trying to remove the splinter from your husband's eye (Matthew 7:3–5).

God's peace is available to you even in the midst of life's chaos.

Wife or Mother?

If all of the challenges we have discussed in this chapter weren't enough to cause difficulties in our marriage, when we add children to the mix, we encounter a completely new set of challenges.

How do we juggle the many hats we wear as a mother? How do I find time for physical intimacy with the challenges of fatigue, nursing, pregnancy, birth control, and children who interrupt? Don't give up hope; we all face the challenges of motherhood with the same feelings of exhaustion and distraction. Is there really sex while I'm raising kids? You bet! In the next chapter we'll look at the realities of motherhood and the practical ways we can keep marriage a priority.

Personal Reflections

1. IDENTIFY two pieces of baggage you carried into your marriage relationship. Commit to opening up those suitcases with the purpose of eventually discarding their contents.

2. THINK back over the past two weeks: Have you reacted to your spouse in a way that was destructive to your marriage? If you could go back and do it over again, how could you have responded rather than reacted?

3. Do you offer a full apology or a half apology when you resolve conflict? The next time a conflict emerges, take ownership of your part by offering a full apology, asking for forgiveness.

For Men Only

When Jill and I married each of us brought our own experiences, beliefs, and thoughts about marriage, parenting, sex, and much more into our marriage. Some of what we carried in was good information and right thinking, while some of what we carried in was based upon negative experience, wrong information, or a lack of good role models to teach us along the way. We refer to these experiences as the "baggage" we carried into the marriage journey.

It is good to examine some of the baggage you carried into marriage. How are your conflict resolution skills? How was the topic of sex handled in the family in which you were raised? How have you allowed the media to affect your thinking on love, sex, and marriage? These questions are just a sampling of the questions we need to ask ourselves to truly evaluate the good and the bad we may be contributing to our marriage.

Take a peek at the subheads in this chapter and pick out one or two sections to read. See if you can discover a few things about yourself. I found that I really had much to learn as a husband and began to make the time to learn more about my wife and God's plan for marriage in general.

Our sexual relationship was sabotaged by the lies I believed from the pornography I had consumed over the years. Our conflict could never find resolution because I was determined to win rather than resolve. Our communication was hindered by my pride. Can you identify with any of these? If so, I encourage you to unpack a few suitcases of your own. If you do, I believe you'll find your marriage at a new level of intimacy!

Mark

chapter 3

And Then I Had Kids

AFTER NOT FEELING WELL for a few days, I decided to pay a visit to the doctor. This flu seemed to be hanging on a little longer than usual. Mark and I had been married just over ten months and this was the first time I'd been sick.

As I explained my symptoms to the doctor, he listened closely, nodding here and there. After I finished, he asked me one simple question, "Do you think you might be pregnant?" I assured him that I didn't see how, because we were very consistent in our birth control. He told me we would start by ruling out pregnancy and then proceed from there.

It wasn't five minutes before he walked back in that room and said, "Mrs. Savage, I believe we've found the problem. You are pregnant." I couldn't believe my ears. Pregnancy had never crossed my mind. Little did I realize how my life, my marriage, and my body would change over the coming months.

Whether you became a mother through pregnancy, marriage, or adoption, you understand what I am talking about. When children come into the picture, many changes take place. The sexual relationship is no exception.

Children bring unique challenges to the marriage relationship. If we don't identify and address these challenges, we will find ourselves swallowed up and overwhelmed by the additional responsibilities. Let's take a look at each of these challenges and discuss some ways of combating their negative impact on the sexual relationship.

Fatigue

When I crawl into bed at night, I rarely find myself suffering from insomnia. On the contrary, most nights I'm asleep before my head hits the pillow. Dishes, laundry, meal preparation, carpool, piano lessons ... it seems to be an endless cycle of responsibility and activity. So much for a little recreation after hours. The physical and emotional energy spent taking care of children is exhausting. After actively playing with my kids, it seems that I have little energy left to play sexually with my husband!

The early years of motherhood are especially taxing. Newborns, infants, and toddlers take an incredible amount of nonstop physical energy. If you add in colic, illness, and/or poor sleeping habits, you have additional stress. Those days I found that once I began moving in the morning, I didn't quit until I crawled into bed at night. I had been touched, tackled, and tumbled all over. I had nursed and nestled my child all day. I had navigated sibling rivalry constantly. Then I would crawl into my bed at night next to a husband who had a gleam in his eye, and I wanted to scream, "If one more person touches my body, I'll lose it!"

> *After actively playing with my kids, it seems that I have little energy left to play sexually with my husband!*

Is this an acceptable way of life? I don't believe so. Fatigue is indeed a challenge of motherhood and plays an important role in a sexual relationship (or lack thereof), but we need to meet the challenge, not succumb to it.

When there is an infant in the house, we often hear the sage advice about sleeping when the baby sleeps. That works very well when there is just one child, but add one or two toddlers to the mix and finding a few minutes to nap seems impossible. Regardless, we do need to find ways to rest. Over the years I have found several strategies to combat fatigue.

Bedtime

I have always been a stickler about my kids' bedtimes, but very lax about my own time for "hitting the sack." There is a strong temptation to stay up late after the kids go to bed. It seems we can't accomplish anything during the day without twenty-five interruptions, so it is tempting to get some late-night reading or project time or just finish household tasks. At the same time, our bodies need rest not only for our own physical health, but also to be the wives and mothers we need to be.

Getting to bed just thirty or sixty minutes earlier can make an incredible difference in our energy levels. Our bodies need the rest. Our children need the patience that comes with our being more rested. And our marriages benefit from the extra energy, both emotionally and physically. Yes, that means we sometimes may go to bed leaving the kitchen a mess or the toys spread across the floor, but a rested, happy mom cleaning up a kitchen beats an exhausted, crabby mom any day (just ask my husband and children if you don't believe me!).

Naps

Several years ago I was the featured guest on a national call-in radio program. One of the callers was a young mother of a six-month-old baby. The woman admitted that she was exhausted. You could hear it in her voice as we spoke about the demands of motherhood. She felt that she couldn't take a nap, because by doing so she wouldn't be "earning her keep" as a homemaker. I explained, on the contrary, that taking a nap on occasion was a part of her job description, because it allowed her to be the wife and mom she needed to be.

It is *so* hard to take a nap when laundry and dishes are calling your name! Yet it is so necessary, especially when we're in the motherhood season of infants and preschoolers. With one child, I could sleep when she slept. When we added another child, it became more difficult. I can remember some desperate days when I would take my two-year-old to bed with me in the afternoon just to be sure she would sleep while the baby slept, so I could sleep as well. Those naps were my lifelines to sanity when the demands of a newborn were robbing me of every ounce of energy.

Sometimes I could only get a nap with the assistance of my husband or a friend. If the exhaustion was too much to bear, I would call Mark before he headed home from work to ask him to consider giving me thirty minutes of shut-eye before the evening shift began. I found this worked much better than meeting him at the door and requesting (or worse, demanding) that he watch the kids. It was honoring to him yet making my needs known.

Sometimes a friend with whom you trade childcare can give you some reprieve from the nonstop demands of small children. You are doubly blessed if that friend is a neighbor. Remember, no one will see your need. You'll need to ask for it when you need it. You and I need to understand the art of self-care.

Sometimes a nap is necessary to give yourself energy for lovemaking later in the evening. Sometimes we need to take a nap for our *marriage*, not just for our children. Your children are worth it, your health is worth it, and your marriage is worth it.

Pregnancy

It is amazing to watch the female human body adjust to meet the needs of a growing, unborn child. As I neared my due date with each baby, my husband would marvel at how skin could stretch so much! While accompanied by joy and excitement, the miracle of pregnancy also brings challenges. As the body changes, the physical relationship of the couple can be affected as well. Certain lovemaking positions are no longer comfortable (or even attainable!). The breasts become more tender. Some women become more self-conscious about their growing bellies. Others find themselves feeling more sensual.

The months of pregnancy can be a wonderful time to be creative with lovemaking. Because likes and dislikes can change from week to week, use this time to become more comfortable with conversing with each other during lovemaking. Capitalize upon this season rather than withdraw.

The emotional roller coaster of pregnancy can also affect our physical relationship. One mom told me that during her pregnancy her husband's work load increased, which meant he had less interest in sex. His lack of intimate advances compounded the negative emotions she was already feeling in terms of a poor body image as she grew bigger and bigger. This is where hinting around simply doesn't work. Sometimes our emotions during pregnancy cause us to be a bit more needy. We can't expect our husbands to figure that out. We need to communicate that our need to know that "he still desires me" often increases during pregnancy.

Intercourse may become more challenging in the later months of pregnancy. In addition to trying different lovemaking positions, use this time to practice the art of pleasuring (see chapter 10). Remember God gave us the sexual relationship in marriage for the purpose of satisfaction, enjoyment, and pleasure.

Nursing

I will always remember my experience of nursing our four children. I loved holding them in my arms and snuggling them up to my breast. Through breastfeeding, a baby's nutritional needs are met and the emotional bonds are strengthened. However, the nursing experience can affect the sexual relationship between a husband and a wife.

I wasn't prepared for that change as a young mother. My breasts, up to that point, had been a part of my feminine shape (yes, it was a small shape, but a shape nonetheless!) and a part of the sexual being God made me. Now they had a completely different function. And during the nursing season I didn't enjoy my breasts being touched in lovemaking. For my dear husband, all of a sudden the rules had changed. Unfortunately, we didn't talk about it. Instead our physical relationship struggled, as I desired to be "left alone."

Some moms experience the same feelings I did. Others report that their desires for breast stimulation during lovemaking actually increased during the season of nursing.

What do you do when nursing a baby changes your physical desires? First, you talk about it with your husband. If you don't talk about it, he may take the change in desire personally, thinking it is about him, especially if your desire is to be touched less. He needs to know that this is just a season. Most likely, after the baby is weaned, your previous desires will return.

Second, become comfortable with your own body. Decide what you like and dislike. Then communicate those preferences in love to your spouse. Don't be afraid to talk about your sexual desires.

A discussion of nursing and the effect it has on the sexual relationship wouldn't be complete without addressing the probability of milk letdown during lovemaking. Most often a milk letdown happens at some point during lovemaking and at the very least when a woman experiences an orgasm. Keeping an extra towel on hand is sometimes a good idea!

Birth Control

When it comes to discussing birth control, the Christian community agrees to disagree. Some denominations believe any form of birth control is unacceptable. Other denominations believe natural methods are allowed. Still others choose to remain silent on the issue and allow couples to make their own choices. Because birth control can affect a couple's love life, I will include a discussion here.

Looking back over the past eighteen years of marriage, I now realize how much birth control challenged our love life. We used a variety of methods: the pill, the diaphragm, NFP (Natural Family Planning), and ultimately we chose a permanent form of birth control with a vasectomy.

Each form had its benefits and drawbacks. The pill made me moody, but it allowed great spontaneity. The diaphragm was a hassle, allowed for no spontaneity, yet it carried no side effects. NFP helped me (and Mark) to know my body and my cycle well, but it was limiting in our physical relationship. The vasectomy has been the most freeing of all the methods we experienced. People said our sexual relationship would improve with the possibility of pregnancy removed from the picture. They were right! At the same time, because it is permanent, it is a big decision to make together as a couple. (Mark was ready to make that decision five years before I was!)

The possibility of pregnancy can hamper the physical relationship in marriage. No matter what form of control you use, you will be faced with weighing out the pros and cons of what is available. If you choose a method that doesn't allow for spontaneity, you will have to plan your lovemaking. If you choose a method with more spontaneity, you may have to deal with some side effects. When researching side effects, make sure to ask about physical side effects such as vaginal dryness or lower sex drive, which could affect your sexual pleasure.

Children

So far we have talked about fatigue, pregnancy, nursing, and birth control. Another challenge is the presence of children in the home. When they are small, their physical demands can be stifling. They may have a habit of crawling into bed with you or knocking on the door at the most inopportune times. The fear of making too much noise may inhibit you.

A lock on the bedroom door is very helpful in providing you privacy and peace of mind from interruptions. This also protects the innocence of your children. One mom says that from the time their children were small, the master bedroom was known as Mom and Dad's "private room." They taught their children never to enter without knocking and asking if they could come in. The kids learned respect for Mom and Dad's privacy at a very young age.

Mark and I thought only small children would influence our love life, but older children can also have a profound effect on your physical relationship. As they enter the teen years, they begin staying up later than you do! Your desire for "time alone" seems to be beyond your grasp.

At that point, it's time to think outside the box. Has lovemaking always been an "after hours" activity? Maybe now it is time to have some "afternoon delight." A long lunch hour, an early evening escapade while the kids are at a ballgame, a middle-of-the-night treat are all ways to beat the challenges of keeping the relationship fun during the childrearing years.

Childbirth

After the birth of each of our four children, the doctor always gave the same instructions: sexual relations can be resumed in six weeks. Mark always said those were the longest six weeks of his life! What no one ever told me, though, is that when sexual relations were resumed after six weeks, it did not necessarily mean it would be pain free. While most of the healing from childbirth takes place during the six-week period, the first few times you make love may necessitate some slow and gentle handling as you resume your physical relationship. If pain continues past the first few love-making sessions following childbirth, you will want to consult your doctor.

Physical Health

Several months after delivering her third child, Jenny found sexual intercourse very painful. She figured it was simply her episiotomy healing more slowly than in the past. After several weeks of pain, she reluctantly visited her doctor—sure that the pain was all in her head.

Upon examination the doctor found that Jenny's vaginal lymph nodes were swollen. Obviously, she had some kind of infection, so he prescribed an antibiotic that worked within a matter of days. Soon Jenny and David's sex life was back to normal.

Have you ever found yourself in Jenny's place? As mothers, we are quick to take our children to the doctor when they experience discomfort, yet we'll wait weeks and even months to seek medical care for ourselves. In Jenny's case, she couldn't have imagined what might be wrong. Her experiences with a lifetime of yeast infections didn't clue her in; these symptoms were different. After her doctor visit she confessed, "I didn't even know I had lymph nodes in my vagina!"

Physical health does affect one's sexual relationship. When was the last time you had an annual physical? Have you had a pap smear and breast exam within the past twelve months? Do you know your cholesterol level? Are you drinking enough water? Eating the right foods?

Last summer I chose to lose some "baby" weight that had accumulated over four pregnancies. After cutting out most of the things I love to eat (French fries, ice cream, brownies, candy bars), I successfully lost seventeen pounds and dropped several clothing sizes. I expected to feel better about myself, but I was surprised at the supplementary benefits. I was unaware of how uncomfortable I had become with the appearance of my body. I had let my health slip, and in doing so I had felt inhibited physically. The extra weight had been sapping my energy as well. When my health improved, our physical relationship improved as well.

Exercise is an area that I struggle with since adding children to our family. I always enjoyed aerobics and managed to take aerobics classes until shortly after our second child was born. Now I find walking to be the most affordable and mom-friendly physical exercise, although I still struggle with making it a regular part of my day. Exercise increases our energy level and keeps our heart and circulation working well. Find some form of exercise that works for you—there are numerous benefits to be had!

Your children and your husband need you to take care of yourself! God gave you a beautiful body that he asks you to care for while you live on this earth. Our bodies come in all sizes and shapes, but they all need good nutrition, an abundance of water, exercise, and regular medical care. Make a commitment today to keep your health near the top of your priority list!

Making the Switch From "Mom" to "Wife"

Many times women talk about a loss of sexual desire after children enter the picture. There are varying reasons for this, and many we have already discussed. The reality is we are spinning a lot of plates. We have a lot on our minds. We are tired. We are stretched to our limits. We feel we have nothing left to give. Yet we can't wait twenty-some years to resume our sexual relationship.

Part of the problem is that most of us try to go from "Mom" to "Sex Goddess" in thirty seconds flat. It doesn't work that way. Our minds and bodies often won't let us do that. We have to have a plan for making the transition. After we determine the plan, we need to put it to action.

There are several ways to make the switch from mom to wife. They are not difficult at all, just strategic in nature. In other words, you have to think about putting them into motion, so the desire and feelings will follow.

Two categories of preparation need to be considered: physical and mental.

Physical Preparation

How we feel about our physical appearance can make a huge difference in our comfort with our sexual relationship in marriage. In his book *The Mystery of Marriage*, Mike Mason notes: "One of the most funda-mental and important tasks that has been entrusted to marriage is the work of reclaiming the body for the Lord, of making pure and clean and holy again that which has been trampled in the mud of shame."[13]

Can you stand in front of a mirror without any clothes on and be comfortable with your nakedness? That is one of the first places to start. We have to be comfortable with the bodies God gave us and with our sexuality in general.

> Part of the problem is that most of us try to go from "Mom" to "Sex Goddess" in thirty seconds flat. It doesn't work that way. We have to have a plan for making the transition.

In his book *In Celebration of Sex*, Dr. Rosenau discusses the importance of learning to love your body. He suggests the following activity:

Stand nude in front of a full-length mirror. Now observe yourself and resist making any judgments. After observing a few minutes, start with your hair and proceed down to your feet and accept and describe every one of your body parts with no negative judgments: "This is my hair, and it is brown with a cowlick." Now observe more closely parts you don't like and verbally make yourself accept them and say something affirming about them:

"God gave me these thighs, and they are strong and support me in many things I enjoy doing."[14]

Another important part of preparing physically includes the practice of good hygiene. A daily bath or shower, brushing your teeth two or three times each day, and shaving regularly can go a long way in feeling comfortable being physically close to your husband.

Do you find yourself uncomfortable with unwanted body hair? I love how Christian author and speaker Liz Curtis Higgs talks about the realities of age when she states that you know you are getting older when you have to start carrying tweezers with your lipstick. I have found that to be so true! I can't believe the big, black hairs that have popped out in all kinds of places on my face and other parts of my body that we'll not mention for now! The truth is, many women are bothered by body hair, which keeps them from feeling sexy. I consulted an esthetician about hair removal to get expert advice. Below you'll find the best ways to handle unwanted body hair.

	Shave	Wax	Pluck	Electrolysis	Depilatory
Facial		X	X	X	X*
Underarms	X	X		X	X
Legs	X	X		X	X
Breasts			X	X	
Bikini Line	X	X	X	X	X

*For facial areas, use specially formulated depilatories.

Some women choose to trim their pubic hair to feel more comfortable with their body as well. Your personal preference is what is most important when it comes to hair removal.

Mental Preparation

They say the mind is the largest sex organ in the body. That is indeed the truth. A look in the Bible helps us understand this. In Song of Solomon 5:4, we read about the beloved waiting for the lover to come home. She says,

"My lover thrust his hand through the latch-opening; my heart began to pound for him."

Can you recall some of the emotions you felt when you were first dating your husband? I met Mark on a blind date just two weeks before I began my freshman year in college. We dated throughout my freshman year and were married the following summer. I remember waiting for his phone call every evening. I remember anticipating the time we would spend together. I remember the excitement building, the closer it got to Friday evening when we would usually go out. After we were engaged, I would stare at my diamond ring for minutes at a time, thinking about the man I loved. Truly, *my heart began to pound for him.* Do you remember some of those emotions?

Fast-forward three, five, seven, or ten years ... whatever brings you to today. Sure, you think about him now and anticipate his arrival home. However, instead of your heart, now it's your head that pounds as you watch the clock counting the minutes until he can come home and *help* you!

Do you see what happens? In the midst of marriage and children, we stop thinking about our husbands. Instead, we start thinking about what they can do for us. We stop thinking about the unique way God has created them, and we start thinking about all the things they do wrong and how they fall short as husbands and fathers. This is a dangerous place to be, and yet most of us arrive there before we even realize it. What can we do to move out of this dangerous, marriage-destroying place? Consider these three strategies:

1. *Take a few minutes to fix yourself up before he comes home from work.* A dear friend gave me this wise counsel early in our marriage. I thought it was for the purposes of appearances, but I also found that it helps greatly with mental preparation. As I pause in my busy day, I think about

Mark. I anticipate him coming home. In just a little way, *my heart begins to pound for him.*

2. *Replace the enemy's lies with God's truth.* In my thirteen years of experience encouraging moms, I have found most women to be very judgmental and critical of their husbands. This man who could do no wrong before marriage can do no right after marriage, and especially after the children come along. I struggled with this greatly. My criticism and harsh judgment were killing our marriage. I finally realized that I was the only person who could make the change here. Instead of looking for behavior changes in my husband, I realized that I needed a heart change for me. As critical thoughts entered my mind about Mark, I replaced them with God's truth about him. It wasn't Mark who needed to change, it was Jill. As I start seeing Mark as who he is in God's eyes, *my heart begins to pound for him.*

3. *Take some time for yourself after the children are in bed.* Another friend gave me this advice, and it has made so much difference in our physical relationship. She asked me to think through what it was that helped me unwind. What disconnected me from "mom" and helped connect me to who I was as a woman, as an individual? Every one of us has something that helps her to unwind. For some, it may be running. For others, it might be reading. For me, I love a warm bath, candlelight, and soft music. I find that when we're looking at some "horizontal fellowship" after the kids are in bed, I'm much more likely to be in the mood if I take some time to unwind, think about who God has created me to be, and ready myself to be with my husband.

Seeing Yourself as a Sexual Being

Another important part of mental preparation is remembering who you are as a sexual being. God created you with sexuality in mind. Yet in the midst of motherhood, it is easy to forget that part of you. Dr. Mark Gentry, an OB/GYN, devotes one evening a month for annual pap/breast exam visits for his patients. On a recent evening, he saw nine patients. Six of the nine patients complained of decreasing sex drives. All six were young women who are in what would be considered the "sexual peak" of their lives. They were also tired, worn-out moms who have completely forgotten who God created them to be as a sexual being.

Transitioning from mom to wife may require a little bit of assistance to get the sexual fires burning again. When Dr. Gentry asks these moms to think about what it is that lights their fires, they don't have an answer. They are so far removed from remembering that part of who they are, they can't even begin to tell what is a turn-on for them.

Do you find yourself here? I know I do many times. Here are some ways to create a spark when the fire seems to be cold:

- Read Song of Solomon in the Bible. This book is a short, poetic book of the Bible that illustrates the emotional and physical relationship of marriage. This is God's sex manual!
- Invest in a good Christian sexual technique book. One I highly recommend is *In Celebration of Sex* by Douglas Rosenau. When you struggle getting "in the mood," read a few pages to serve as a reminder of God's plan for the sexual relationship in marriage. This book needs to have its permanent home on the bedside table (yet safe from the eyes of children).

- Pick up *Simply Romantic Nights* published by Family Life (www.familylife.com). This box of creative romantic ideas helps to get the fire burning again.
- Pay attention to the subtle sexual cues in your body. When I started doing this, I noticed that the few times I had any thoughts about sex were never at night—but almost always during the day. Let me tell you these were fleeting thoughts, but thoughts nonetheless. After I shared this fact with Mark, he began to come home for lunch on occasion!
- Focus on bringing pleasure to your husband, rather than being in the mood yourself. I found that when I take the focus off myself, I am more likely to relax. The mood often follows.

Keep the Marriage a Priority

Take time to care for your body. Take pride in the beautiful, sexual body that God has given you. Purposefully think of your sexual self. Identify strategies that move you from mom to wife more easily.

While you and I might want to push "pause" on the marriage button during the childbearing and childrearing years, we cannot succumb to the temptation. Building intimacy in our marriage must be a priority during these years. How do we do that? Turn to the next chapter and let's find out.

Personal Reflections

1. IDENTIFY one change in your personal habits (eating, sleeping, etc.) that you would like to make to improve your energy for lovemaking. Identify how and when you could make the change.

༄

2. WHEN switching from "mom" to "wife," do you need more mental or physical preparation? Name one strategy you would like to incorporate to help you move from making meat loaf to making love.

For Husbands Only

Although you and I are usually able to focus on physical intimacy whenever we want, our wives are more easily distracted by the responsibilities of home and children. Sometimes it's a challenge for them to make the switch from "mom" to "wife."

Early in our marriage, I discovered a book by Dr. Kevin Leman, entitled *Sex Begins in the Kitchen*. I thought, *This is the book I've been looking for! We need more variety in our sex life, and the kitchen is a great place to start!* When I started reading the book I found that although the author addressed creative sexual encounters, his premise was that sex begins in the kitchen when a husband is supportive and involved in family life and household chores. His help in the kitchen, or with the children, speaks love to his wife, who then feels valued and is more open to the expression of physical love.

Jill came home from her moms' group one day and confirmed this further. In their small group they had discussed what kept the fires of passion burning. What activity drew them closer and helped her feel connected to him? Each mom shared that she felt physically attracted to her husband when he helped with dinner, lent a hand with folding laundry, or assisted with the children's bedtime routines. Yes, that means you emptying the dishwasher is foreplay for her!

Now you and I have to be careful here. Our wives can smell manipulation a mile away. Our goal is not to assist our wives hoping to get sex, but rather to serve them in such a way that they know that they are valued and loved. Our goal needs to be to love them with all of our hearts.

If you haven't been attentive to your wife's needs, start today. Ask her how you might be able to help her more. Discover what fans the flames of passion in her. Maybe it used to be flowers and chocolate, but I have a hunch — now that children have entered the scene — it is more like time, attention, and a little bit of help around the house.

Mark

part 3

The Practical Tools—Outside the Bedroom

chapter 4

Intimacy Builders

WHEN COUPLES STRUGGLE with their sexual relationship they often jump to the conclusion that they are either sexually incompatible or that they need sexual counseling. Although this is certainly the case sometimes, more often sexual intimacy isn't the problem at all. What happens inside the bedroom is a direct reflection of what happens outside the bedroom. When looking to improve the sexual relationship of a marriage, we have to first look to improve our emotional relationship.

Do you remember the definition of intimacy introduced in chapter 1? "Into me see": knowing someone. When we experience emotional intimacy in marriage, there is a natural progression to physical intimacy. When we know one another through the nakedness of our emotions, we desire to know one another through the nakedness of our bodies. That is God's design for intimacy in marriage. He desires for us to experience emotional oneness, which leads to physical oneness.

So in the midst of diapers, dishes, and soccer games, how do we find emotional oneness? How do we deepen our intimacy level outside the bedroom? Intimacy builders help us communicate, connect emotionally, and make the marriage a priority.

Kitchen Time

Evening Scenario

Mark came home from work at his usual arrival time at 5:30 P.M. As he walked through the kitchen, he said hello and gave me a quick peck on the cheek. He changed his clothes, and then began the "look what I did at school today" routine with the kids. While opening the mail, he told me about a few things that had happened at work throughout the day. As I finished up dinner, he began wrestling on the floor with our two younger children.

As we sat down to eat, everyone vied for his or her chance to talk. Each child shared about his or her day, school projects, and friends. Mark and I attempted to get a word in when we could. When we finished dinner, we as a family cleared the table and cleaned up the kitchen. Mark soon disappeared outside to work on a building project in our shed. I found myself growing frustrated as the evening progressed. Once again, I was left to watch the kids, oversee homework, give baths, and move things along toward bedtime. What I had really hoped to do was to run to Wal-Mart to pick up a few items, but that was obviously not going to happen now.

When Mark came in later that evening, I found myself angry with him. Because of our lack of communication, we were now facing an argument and hurt feelings. Had either one of us desired to make love that evening, that spouse would have faced an uphill battle because of our lack of intimacy outside the bedroom.

What Is Kitchen Time?

Making love begins in the actions of both spouses outside the bedroom. Communication is a key ingredient in building intimacy. With all the demands children bring within the home, communication is often one of the first things to go. We have to be intentional in our pursuit of communication or it simply will not happen. That's where kitchen time makes a difference!

Kitchen time is an intentional plan to set aside time to talk. Specifically, it is a time to talk through your expectations for the evening, as well as a time to reconnect after being apart for the day. It is a time to share thoughts, fears, and struggles. It is a time to strategize schedules. More than anything, it is a time to build intimacy.

My friend Mary and her husband, Harry, do their kitchen time right after dinner each evening. This works well with Harry's work schedule. According to Mary, if they have evening plans or activities, he phones her before coming home and they have their kitchen time over the phone.

Kitchen time at the Savage household takes place each weekday when Mark comes home from work. He comes in, changes his clothes, and then joins me at the kitchen island for about fifteen minutes. (During the summer we enjoy the porch swing.) Often he'll have a cup of coffee and I'll have a cup of tea. Then we talk. We talk about his day. We talk about my day. Then we ask each other one very important question: What do you need tonight?

Evening Scenario: Take 2

Let me replay for you the evening I described earlier—this time with kitchen time in place. We will see the impact this intimacy builder can make.

Mark came home from work at his usual arrival time at 5:30 P.M. As he walked through the kitchen, he said hello and gave me a quick peck on the cheek. He changed his clothes and assured the kids he would look at the school papers after Mom and Dad had their kitchen time.

Joining me at the kitchen island, we sat down and took a few moments to communicate eye to eye about our day. Then I asked Mark, "So what do you need tonight?" He said he had hoped to work on his project in the shed, because he was close to finishing it.

He then asked me, "What do you need tonight?" I told him that I needed to go to Wal-Mart *unaccompanied*. Now knowing each other's desires for the evening, we began to strategize how we could make them happen. Mark said, "If I can work on my project until 7:30, that would give me a good chunk of time. At 7:30, send one of the kids out to alert me of the time, and then I'll come inside. I'll assume responsibilities for the evening routine and pick up wherever you are at the time. You can then head to Wal-Mart to get the things you need to purchase."

Wow! What a difference fifteen minutes can make! Now, if either one of us desired to make love later that evening, the emotional intimacy was in place to allow the physical intimacy to happen. We both felt valued and cared for as people. We were operating as a team. We were intentionally working to communicate. We were building intimacy outside the bedroom, and we were setting the stage for a relationship that flourishes inside the bedroom.

Suggestions for Establishing Kitchen Time

Now how do you make kitchen time happen in a house full of children? Here are some suggestions for establishing this in your home:

1. Discuss with your spouse the value of doing kitchen time—enhanced communication, strategizing the evening's activities, and allowing the kids to see you positively and intentionally communicating.
2. Decide when it could take place in your schedule. It is important to schedule your time while the kids are awake; this gives them a sense of security in seeing Mom and Dad making their relationship a priority.

3. Talk to your kids about the new routine you will be establishing. Explain to them that Mom and Dad haven't had the opportunity for good communication time, but your family will be doing things differently now. Establish and enforce the rule that you are not to be interrupted unless it involves blood or death. Explain that after Mom and Dad have their time, you will wrestle with them, look at their school papers, and listen to their stories.

4. Smaller children can be encouraged to play at your feet, but refrain from allowing them to sit on your lap. Be firm about this being Mom-and-Dad time.

5. Allow for some time to adjust to the new routine. Teach and reinforce the standard. After the routine is established, invoke consequences if your kitchen time is not respected.

Why is kitchen time so important? Author and speaker Gary Ezzo explains the value of "couch time," a similar concept taught in the Growing Kids God's Way parenting classes, as a way of providing the children with a visual sense of togetherness. It provides them security as they know that mom and dad are a team working together for the good of the family.

Kitchen time builds intimacy on a daily basis. It increases communication. And more than anything else, it sets the stage for a vibrant love life.

Three-Question Technique

Listening is one of the most important intimacy-building communication gifts that God has given couples. It has often been said that listening is so important to God that he gave us one mouth and two ears. He wants us to listen to one another.

Too often we listen to correct, to make a point, to interrupt, or to eventually talk about ourselves. But we must learn to listen to hear what our spouses are saying, as well as to hear what they are feeling! When we listen to one another, we build intimacy. Remember, "into-me-see" can only happen when we take the time to *see* into another's life. Listening allows us to do just that.

How often do you talk with your spouse only to turn the conversation to your agenda? Instead, try using the three-question technique to help you move away from that intimacy-robbing habit. Basically, the three-question technique is asking three questions before saying anything about yourself. Bobbie and Myron Yagel explain this in their book *15 Minutes to Build a Stronger Marriage*, "With this technique we listen intently enough to be able to ask three questions before we say 'I' or before we switch the conversation to our perspective, interests, or problems." Our goal is to keep the attention focused on the speaker. Here are three attempts Mark and I made at a conversation to illustrate the three-question technique:[15]

Attempt #1

Mark: "I had a great day today!"
Jill: "That's nice. I had a very challenging afternoon with the kids."

Oops! I just flunked the "three-question technique." I said "I" without asking Mark even one question. I used the subject introduced by Mark as a springboard to talk about my day.

Attempt #2

Mark: "I had a great day today!"
Jill: "That's good. What made it so good?"
Mark: "We accomplished so much on the renovation project today, and we were able to get everything cleaned up and ready for tomorrow."

Jill: "Cleaned up? I feel like I have no time to clean up around here. In fact, that was part of my challenge this afternoon."

Oops! One question is making progress, but let's try again.

Attempt #3

Mark: "I had a great day today!"

Jill: "That's good. What made it so good?" (Question 1 asks for more details.)

Mark: "We accomplished so much on the renovation project today, and we were able to get everything cleaned up and ready for tomorrow."

Jill: "That's wonderful. So who was there to help with the project?" (Question 2, a question that says, "Keep talking; I'm interested.")

Mark: "Well, there were probably twenty people who volunteered today. Their experience and commitment to this project helped us accomplish all that we did."

Jill: "Given the challenges and the magnitude of this project, I know this was important to you." (Question 3: Although this wasn't really a question, it was a statement that invited further conversation.)

Mark: "Yes, it was important to me. I am so excited to see it all begin to pay off. I was really beginning to wonder if it was even worth the effort. Now I know we will finish on schedule, and I can relax."[16]

Do you see how much deeper into conversation we were able to go? Now when I begin to talk about my day, the conversation is at a more meaningful, personal level. By drawing each other out and *listening,* we are able to take communication to the next level. We miss learning about one another when we jump in with our own agenda. When we draw each other out in conversation, we find the intimacy we are seeking.

Reconnection

The Big Picture

Spouses who travel pose a different kind of challenge to building intimacy. Because their daily time together is nonexistent or occurs in a phone conversation, they often find themselves feeling disconnected. When the spouse returns home, the couple struggles with physical intimacy because of the distance they have experienced. It is not a hopeless challenge, though. Understanding the concept of reconnection helps light the fires of emotional intimacy that need to be burning in the marriage relationship. Reconnection is strategically planning a time to connect emotionally after being apart for a time.

Whether your spouse is away for an evening or weeks at a time, intentional reconnection is key to building intimacy. Let's look at my friends Doris and Charlie to further illustrate the reconnection process.

Charlie has a job that takes him away from the home for weeks at a time. During one of his many travel assignments, I chatted with Doris over a cup of tea. She talked about how difficult it was when Charlie returned home. She shared that often she felt distant from him. Eventually, we talked about their differing sexual expectations they faced when he returned home. Our conversation went something like this:

Doris: "Charlie is coming home this weekend. I've missed him so much I can hardly wait. At the same time, I hate it when he comes home."

Me: "Why?"

Doris: "Do you know what the first thing is on his mind? He's talking about sex before he's even home! It's not that I don't want to have sex; I just can't go there immediately! We haven't seen each other for weeks!"

Me: "Doris, are you familiar with the concept of reconnection?"

Doris: "No, what's that?"

Me: "Reconnection is the intentional plan to reconnect as a husband and wife emotionally, before you reconnect physically. It's a time to reconnect in your marriage before he is thrust back into the role of hands-on daddy. It's a necessary intimacy builder when you have been apart for a time. Try this: When Charlie comes home this Friday, meet him at the airport."

Doris: "I don't ever meet him at the airport. He leaves his car there!"

Me: "You're not meeting him for logistical purposes but to build intimacy. Meet him and take a half hour to get a piece of pie at an airport restaurant. Fill each other in on the details of the trip, details of home, and talk about plans for the first few days at home. Then see how the rest of your weekend goes."

Well, I didn't hear from Doris until Sunday, when she told me about her wonderful weekend. She said it was the best weekend they had experienced since her husband began traveling. And she said that the physical relationship naturally flowed out of their reconnection date. Because they had connected emotionally, they were able to connect physically! It was a winning strategy.

Although Mark and I don't do a lot of overnight travel, we do find ourselves apart several times during the year. We have learned that purposeful reconnection is a major component of keeping the intimacy fires burning.

Tips for Reconnecting

Here are some tips for making it work:

1. Plan your reconnection date before you return home. If I am going to speak at a conference on Friday and Saturday, we'll plan for a date either Saturday evening or Sunday afternoon. Arranging for childcare and setting the date ahead of time assures us of making it happen.

2. If you don't have the finances to go out, ask a friend or extended family member to watch the kids at their home, while you enjoy a few hours of quiet in the privacy of your own home. Let the answering machine answer the phone, fix your favorite meal, and enjoy some time discussing what you did while you were apart from each other.

3. Use the three-question technique to take the conversation to a deeper level. Make it a point to listen as well as talk.

When you think about it, kitchen time is really a form of reconnection. By strategically planning for staying connected and investing in your relationship—whether you've been apart several hours or several days—you are setting the stage for a marriage that goes the distance.

Date Nights

When Mark and I first met, we purposefully spent time together. Our culture calls this "dating," and most of us mistakenly believe it is useful only until the wedding day; however, married couples need to continue dating throughout their wedded life in order to keep their relationship a priority. If we don't continue dating, we begin to operate as roommates rather than lovers. We may then find ourselves feeling unappreciated and unloved.

Mark and I have found there are three types of dates that are important to our marriage. I want to explore all three and how to make them happen in the midst of the childrearing years.

Daily Dates

These dates are the little acts of love and appreciation we show for each other every day. A hug in the morning. A passionate kiss in the afternoon. A note tucked in a briefcase. A phone call in the middle of the day just to touch base. A lipstick message written on the bathroom mirror. Kitchen time. These are all daily dates, and they are essential to a healthy marriage. They take nothing more than effort and thoughtfulness, yet their benefit is invaluable.

Weekly or Biweekly Dates

These dates are planned outings without children. Just like the dates before we were married, these dates are planned, purposeful times spent together. Usually consisting of several hours alone, weekly or biweekly outings help us to focus on each other without the distraction of being a hands-on parent at the same time. They give us time to talk, share, strategize, dream, and plan for the future. They give us much needed eye-to-eye communication.

Dates don't have to cost money. There are creative ways to spend time together that don't require money. Here are a few to get you started: pack a picnic and go to a park, take a drive in the country, or ask a friend to watch the kids so you and your husband can enjoy your favorite homemade meal in your own home. Have fun thinking of inexpensive dates you and your spouse will enjoy!

An occasional movie is fine, but be careful about considering the movie theater a good date idea. A movie date does not allow for communication, and it does very little to deepen intimacy. If you do include a movie in your date, try to also include dinner or dessert in your plans to allow for time to talk.

Annual Dates

Annual dates are the getaways every marriage needs. These overnights are designed to keep the romance in the relationship. Mark and I find that these are the times that help us remember who we are as a couple—not as mom and dad. They also help us recall the very things that attracted us to one another in the first place. Getaways instill a sense of fun and spontaneity in a marriage relationship. They also go a long way in building intimacy for a long-lasting relationship.

Annual getaways can be anything from one night alone in a local hotel to a weeklong vacation for just the two of you. We have found that both types of getaways have been important to our marriage. A twenty-four-hour rendezvous has a way of allowing for an escape from the daily routine to focus on each other. Several days away allows for a time of exploration together. It is an opportunity to relax and become reacquainted.

Of course, there are challenges inherent with dating. If we can think through the challenges ahead of time, we are on our way to incorporate dates into our marriage relationship.

Scheduling Challenges

We are busy people. We have work, church, and volunteer responsibilities that require our time. If our children are older, their activities scream for our attention. When can we possibly fit in "dating" again?

The days will fill up naturally. This means we can't wait until we have a "free night" and then think we'll take advantage of it. We are fooling ourselves if we really believe this will happen. It won't.

In looking at scheduling challenges, we have to be proactive—looking ahead, strategizing, and planning our time together. Then we have to put it on the calendar in indelible ink and schedule upcoming events around it. The time together becomes sacred; except for emergencies (illness, injury, etc.), the date is protected from the infringement of other activities.

This becomes difficult at times. The world will demand that we make other choices. There will be the temptation to work late—just to finish a project. There will be the temptation to cancel because we're tired. There will be the temptation to take advantage of those basketball tickets that someone just offered you—when the game falls on your date night. It all comes down to priorities.

What earthly relationship is the *most important relationship* in the family? Your marriage. It is time we make our decisions based on our priorities. It's time to start talking and start making it happen.

Yes, scheduling challenges will happen. That's why it is important to discuss these questions:

1. When can we connect each day?
2. What time during the week can we reserve for a date?
3. What plans do we need to be making for some getaway time this year?

Don't get drawn down the road of passivity when it comes to your marriage. Face the scheduling challenges head-on and make private time happen. Your marriage is worth it!

Financial Challenges

The costs of raising children seem to sap the financial resources of even the most financially savvy families. It is possible to find some funds to invest in your marriage, but it helps to plan ahead, incorporate a strategy, and budget some finances to invest in your marital relationship. Consider setting aside a predetermined amount of money each paycheck. A Christmas fund allows you to save for gift purchases during the Christmas season. Similarly, a getaway fund allows you to save for an annual marriage getaway. Don't forget to budget money for monthly childcare expenses if you need to hire a babysitter for your weekly or biweekly dates.

> What earthly relationship is the most important relationship in the family? Your marriage.

Not finding any room in your budget for marriage monies? What might you give up that would allow you to loosen up some funds? Eating out for lunch? Soft drinks? Prepackaged snacks? Think about the long-term investment you are making and adjust your spending to reflect your priorities.

Childcare Challenges

Finding someone to care for the children is often the biggest challenge for many couples. Over the years Mark and I have found several ways to meet the childcare challenge. Here are some possibilities to consider:

Extended Family

Many families have grandparents who live nearby. An evening at Grandma and Grandpa's house once a week or every other week can be a special treat for the kids. In the case of an annual getaway, grandparents or aunts and uncles may be able to come to your home to help keep the normal routine in motion. At other times, a getaway at Grandma's house promises lots of fun!

Trade Sitting

For almost ten years, the only way Mark and I could make date nights a reality was by trading with another couple. It was a simple arrangement: We agreed to watch their children an evening one week in exchange for childcare for our children one evening the next week. We really liked this arrangement for several reasons. First, it didn't cost us anything financially. Second, I always felt more comfortable leaving a baby in the care of another mom. Third, we often found that we could have longer dates than if we were paying a sitter by the hour.

Where can you find another couple who would be willing to trade childcare? Church, school, neighbors, and extended family are all possibilities. We have always tried to find another family with children close in age to our children. We also look for a common parenting philosophy and values.

Paid Sitter

Find a regular sitter to come to your home once a week or once every other week for your date night. Teenagers and college students are often looking for sitting jobs to earn spending money. A regular schedule allows for the habit to be set and calendars to stay clear.

When going away for an overnight, consider asking a young married couple without children to come to your home and stay with your kids. A single college student is also a good candidate for getaway childcare. Pay them a daily rate rather than an hourly rate.

Wrap-Up

It is tempting to let the marital relationship run on autopilot. Time, energy, and sometimes even money are necessary to keep the marriage flames burning. Often it is a hassle to make arrangements for the kids, pack the diaper bag or suitcases if an overnight is on the agenda, and arrange for care in your absence. But it is a hassle that comes with a huge benefit: marriage intimacy in the midst of the childrearing years.

We cannot wait until children leave home to invest in our marriages. We have to do it now—for ourselves and for them. If not, we'll wake up next to our spouses in twenty years and ask, "Who are you?" By investing now, we prevent bankruptcy later.

What happens inside the bedroom *is* a reflection of what happens outside the bedroom. Commit today to incorporate kitchen time into your afternoon. Make it a point to ask three questions of your spouse each time he shares something about himself. Plan for reconnection dates after you've been apart for a time. Finally, return to dating your spouse. Love each other by being thoughtful daily. Go out weekly or biweekly. And get away at least once a year for an overnight.

Looking to improve your love life? Start today by incorporating some intimacy builders into your marriage every single day. As you do so, you will find you are building a firm, marriage-centered foundation for your family. And that's the next strategy we're going to look at!

Personal Reflections

1. How can you make kitchen time a part of your daily routine? Strategize with your husband how to incorporate some eye-to-eye communication when he comes home from work.

2. Do you cut off your spouse during his communication time? For the next twenty-four hours, keep track of how often you turn the conversation to focus on you. Ask God to help you find the self-control to keep the interest focused on your spouse.

3. WHAT evening would work best for your date night? What childcare arrangements work best for you? Set up the arrangements today to make dating a part of your marriage again!

For Husbands Only

Whether you believe it or not, sex really does begin outside the bedroom. I have been amazed at the difference making the marital relationship a priority and investing time and energy into our nonsexual relationship has made in our love life.

This is one chapter I encourage you to read together. Take four nights this week and each night read one section of the chapter. It will probably take you a few minutes to read a section. Then invest a few minutes in your marriage to talk together about how to incorporate these ideas into your relationship on a regular basis.

Investment outside the bedroom pays dividends inside the bedroom!

Mark

chapter 5

Who Am I? Mother or Lover?

STEVE AND ANNIE CHAPMAN wrote and recorded a song about a less-than-ideal, empty-nest marriage. Titled *Who Are You?* the song tells the story of a husband and wife who watch their last child leave home. When they wake up in the morning, they look at one another and ask, "Who are you?" All the years of investing only in the children had robbed them of the intimacy of their marriage.

What an eye-opening message about the importance of investing in the marital relationship in the childrearing years. This is a lesson I had to learn the hard way—after some damage was done that required my immediate attention. I had focused my attention on caring for the needs of my children to the detriment of my marriage. The lack of attention to my husband's needs were eroding our relationship.

We live in a child-centered society. There are positives and negatives to this national obsession. What parent doesn't want to give his child everything possible? Time, energy, material possessions, and opportunities . . . the list is endless. We want to give them the best. We want to provide for them in the best way possible. But did you know the greatest gift you can give a child is a healthy marriage?

A loving, strong, healthy marriage is what will provide children the stability they long for in their young lives. A child's world is greatly defined by the family unit in which the child lives. Mom and Dad define that world. And when Mom and Dad are okay, the child's world is okay. This is the best gift we can give our children. Not only that—it is the best gift we can give our marriage and our love life.

So how do we make our family marriage-centered? It is not a difficult concept to grasp, but it begins with a shift in thinking. Let's examine the traits that define a marriage-centered family.

We Are a Team

It is amazing how quickly our children learn the manipulating tactic of divide and conquer. This is when they find they can get their way by running to one parent in an effort to get the answer they didn't get from the other parent. We also see this tactic in motion when we disagree with each other in the presence of our children. When we allow ourselves to fall for the divide-and-conquer routine, we are operating out of child-centeredness.

A marriage-centered approach operates with a "we are a team" mind-set. A united front is top priority. Mark and I sometimes find we disagree about parenting decisions. But those discussions are reserved for a private, parents-only setting. We both state our feelings about the situation, and then we agree on a plan of action. Often it requires cooperation—a sense of "meeting in the middle." Most important, though, we ultimately present a united response to the child. It's not "Dad said . . . " or "Mom said . . ." It is always "We decided . . ."

I remember one particular discipline incident that came up when we had a houseful of company. We knew we needed to determine an initial plan of action for handling a child's disobedience. The only room in our home that wasn't occupied was a small downstairs bathroom. I smiled at Mark and asked him if he would like to join me in my "office." We closed the door behind us, discussed what had happened, and strategized the appropriate discipline. When we exited our makeshift office a few minutes later, we had agreed upon a plan of action. We were both a part of the decision process. And we were operating as a team.

How does the "we are a team" concept affect our love life? It has a huge effect on the way we feel toward one another. If I feel that my partner is always undermining me, I don't feel loved and valued. Trust is also broken in a divide-and-conquer parenting maneuver. Trust, love, and a sense of value are essential elements in a loving, physical relationship. Marriage-centered, not child-centered. Do you see how what happens outside the bedroom, in *all* areas of life, affects our relationship inside the bedroom?

Invest Now!

The childrearing years are some of the busiest of our lives. Life moves at such a breakneck speed that we often sense chaos in our homes. There is laundry to do, meals to make, an income to earn, carpools to run, soccer games to attend—it's all so overwhelming at times! Am I suggesting that in the midst of all this we need to invest in our marriage as well? Yes, that's exactly what I'm saying! It's an investment that will pay dividends for years to come.

Consider the Steve and Annie Chapman song I described at the beginning of this chapter. It depicts a marital relationship that has deteriorated due to a lack of investment. The couple's life revolved around their children. As they enter the empty-nest season of their lives, they find themselves with little in common. Because they neglected to invest in the childrearing years of their marriage, they were suffering the consequences of their poor choices. "Who are you?" is the question before them. "I don't know you. I thought I did, but now that we remove the common link we shared (the children) I find that I don't really know you."

You and I hold the opportunity to learn from this couple's mistake. We must make the decision to be husbands and wives first and moms and dads second. We must commit the time, energy, and resources *now* to invest in our relationships—to be reminded of who we are as couples.

We need to decide to date *now*, even when it is a hassle to do so. We need to decide to improve our communication skills *now*, even with busy schedules. We need to determine to make the marriage the foundational relationship in the family *now*, even when the world disagrees.

Investing in the marital relationship is a winning strategy for success in the bedroom as well. As each partner feels valued by the other, trust and emotional intimacy increases in the relationship. That's what makes the marriage investment a worthwhile endeavor!

Priority Power!

Every day we make choices that reflect our priorities. Often the choices are subconscious rather than conscious determinations. In fact, most of our choices are based on the urgent rather than the important things in our life.

We in a marriage-centered family must keep the important things *important*. We must identify the urgent things that are stealing our marriage. We also must identify the difference between "good" and "best" choices and incorporate our true priorities into the decisions we make.

During this season of our marriage, Mark and I have our weekly date on Friday afternoons. With all our children in school, this time works well for us. In the past ten years we've reserved Saturday afternoons, Sunday evenings, or a weeknight for our time together. Each year, we've had to reevaluate or adjust our schedule depending on our responsibilities and our kids' activities. It's been tempting to not commit to have a date each week, but we know the damage that will result if we grow slack. Instead, we've worked to keep our priorities straight. We've had to make hard decisions at times.

Mark is a pastor. People need him all the time. There have been many occasions someone has wanted to meet with him on a Friday afternoon—the *only* time they can meet. It's been hard for him to set the boundaries, but he's learned he must for our marriage.

In truth, there is always something that is trying to steal our time together. Because of that, we have to keep our priorities in place. This is where understanding the difference between urgent and important is imperative. The urgent is all the people who need him, but these people will come and go in his life. The *important* is our marriage relationship. This relationship is designed to last a lifetime.

The concept of good and best is also helpful to understand here. It would be a *good* use of Mark's time to meet with whomever needs him that day. They would certainly be encouraged and helped during that time. However, since his marriage needs to be the priority, what is *best* is to keep our relationship a priority.

Don't get me wrong here: There are times when a true emergency arises on a Friday afternoon, and we have to deal with it. What we're talking about here is identifying the little demands (which we often see as big demands) that continue to rob you of your marriage and your time together.

Teach Marital Respect

Having a wide span in the ages of our children has had its drawbacks and its benefits. One of the benefits is the parenting education we experienced. Anne and Evan were two years apart and then there was a four-year span before Erica came along. It was another five years before Austin entered the scene.

One of the concepts we've learned in our seventeen-year span of parenting is that parenting is really about leadership. It's casting a vision for your children. Taking them from Point A to Point B. Imparting wisdom. Building character. It is also modeling for them how to live their lives. Ultimately, it is the privilege of ushering them into adulthood.

In the early parenting years, we missed opportunities to teach and lead. Far more often we parented in times of conflict, rather than led and taught our children in times of non-conflict. One area we changed, when we had a little bit more experience under our belt, was teaching our children about respecting the marital relationship.

Children need to know that the marriage relationship is important. They need to know that it is something to be protected. They have to be shown how to prioritize the relationship. They need to understand privacy needs for Mom and Dad.

Teach your children to respect your marriage. Make it a part of the DNA of your family. Here are some practical ways to do this:

1. *Invest in your own private space.* Several years ago Mark inherited a little bit of money when his Grandma Carroll passed away. We decided to take that money and invest in our bedroom. We purchased a small love seat and ottoman, a side table with a lamp, a new comforter for our bed, and some pretty pillows. This transformed our bedroom into a special room for the two of us. It doesn't require a lot money, however, to make your room special. Simply adding some candles, a dimmer switch on your overhead light, a CD player for some romantic music, and framed pictures of the two of you will do the trick!

2. *Teach your children about adult time.* There are many times when Mom and Dad need to talk or

spend uninterrupted time together in their own home. Teaching children about adult time, and what is expected during that time, is key here. The kitchen time mentioned in the previous chapter is a perfect example of adult time.

3. *Be affectionate as a couple.* Every couple has to determine the level of affection they are comfortable with. At the Savage household, Mark and I are very affectionate in the presence of our children. We hold hands, cuddle on the couch, and often are found hugging and kissing in the kitchen. Usually we hear from the kids, "Mom and Dad are at it again!" or they'll pretend that they are disgusted by it and hide their eyes. In reality, they love it and it models the importance of the marital relationship to them.

Bedtime and Sleeping Arrangements

When Anne and Evan were small, it seemed they more often slept in our bed than in their own. No wonder our sexual relationship was struggling—our child-centeredness was robbing us of our needed privacy.

When Erica and Austin came along, we put boundaries in place to keep our bedroom off limits to sleeping children. We changed our parenting approach and found that our children were much more secure with the priority of our marriage in first place. Because of this, both Erica and Austin slept through the night at much earlier ages than Anne or Evan did.

If your children are sleeping in your bed, it's time to make a change. With the exception of a terrible nightmare or an occasional snuggling during a thunderstorm, Mom and Dad's bed needs to be just that. When we made this switch in our home, I learned to depend on a baby monitor (or two!) to keep me tuned in to my infant's or toddler's needs in the bedroom down the hall.

Evaluating bedtime and the bedtime routine can also have a profound effect on your marriage. When our third child came along, we stopped lying down with our kids to put them to sleep. It took some retraining (for us and for them!), but was well worth the effort. Children need to learn how to put themselves to sleep. This is part of understanding the job of leadership as a parent. By the time we added Austin to our family, we put him in his crib awake and allowed him to learn to fall asleep on his own. What a stress relief this was for our marriage and our family!

If you need to make some changes, make sure to reframe them for your children. Don't just change the rules on them—bring them along by communicating the changes that will be taking place. When we decided to change our bedtime routine, we talked about it at dinner one night and regularly in the following weeks. We explained why we were going to make changes, when it would start, how it would look, and what would happen if they were disobedient to the new standard. We also allowed a grace period of a couple weeks to allow them to adjust to the change before we responded with consequences. It took some energy to make the change, and certainly there were some tears in the process, but in the end it was well worth the effort. It's a better deal for them because they are getting the rest they need and we are getting the time we need.

When David and Claudia Arp wrote an article for *Christian Parenting Today* entitled "Love Life for the Very Married Parent," one mom who got it right wrote a letter to the editor:

> My husband and I just celebrated our fifth wedding anniversary. We have a three-and-a-half-year-old daughter and another child on the way. The scenarios described in your article are foreign to us; we have had no problems maintaining a good marriage and sex life after the arrival of children.

We put our daughter to bed at 8:00 P.M. each night. My husband and I do not retire until 10:00 P.M. This leaves us two hours of peace, quiet, and togetherness each night. We have taught our daughter right from the beginning that once she is in bed, she stays in bed. She is strong-willed, but we have no trouble maintaining peace at bedtime, because this routine is strictly enforced and she has learned that it does no good to fight it. My husband and I are able to look forward to the last two hours of each day. We have time to sit and talk, enjoy our hot tub, watch a movie together, or be romantic.[17]

Now, there's a couple who understands that they are the parents, they are in charge, they need their time, and their consistency will pay off. They love their child enough to give her boundaries. When our parenting perspective is balanced, our children and our marriage reap the benefits!

At the Savage home, Tuesday and Thursday nights are early-to-bed nights. This means the two younger children are in bed between 8 P.M. and 8:30 P.M., which they are most nights, and our teenagers are in their room by 9 P.M., which they are not most nights. This is one way we have taught our teenagers to respect the marital relationship. It took a little while for Anne and Evan to learn to manage their time and their homework to be ready to be in their rooms by 9 P.M. With our computer in the kitchen, they would often be up until 10 P.M. or 11 P.M. writing papers, doing research, and most often Instant Messaging their friends (most kids don't talk on the phone these days—they talk on the computer!). However, on Tuesday and Thursday nights, they have to think about Mom and Dad's needs before their own. While they don't have to go right to bed (although sometimes they do), they use the time to finish homework, read, or listen to music. In the end, they have learned to value the quiet time in their room as much as the investment Mom and Dad are making in their marriage.

Bob Barnes, author of *Great Sexpectations,* shares a story about a time when he and his wife wanted to have an evening to themselves in the family room. He told their teenage daughter that she didn't have to go to sleep, but she had to be in her room by 9 P.M. She argued a bit and asked, "What will happen if I come into the family room after 9:00?" Her dad answered, "You'll see two naked bodies in front of the fireplace!"[18]

Maybe that reply seems a little shocking to you, but the point remains the same. You and I are not bad parents when we insist on time alone. In fact, we're teaching our children a lesson that will strengthen their own marriages someday. For children, limits equals love. Placing limits, establishing boundaries, and setting expectations speak volumes of love to our growing children.

Our four children love to snuggle in bed with us on Saturday mornings, and I love fitting all six of us in our king-size waterbed and listening to the giggles. There are certainly occasions when I snuggle with our children in their beds at night as they pour out their hearts or share things that are bothering them. And on occasion Anne or Evan need help with their homework on a Tuesday or Thursday night after 9 P.M. However, I'm glad we've learned the value of putting boundaries in place that invest in our marriage and provide emotional security for our children.

Wife First, Mother Second

In my book *Professionalizing Motherhood,* I devoted an entire chapter to the concept of being a wife first and mother second. This was a lesson God taught me eleven years into our marriage. An unexpected all-expense paid trip to Rome, Italy, for Mark and me was the tool God used to show me my error of child-centeredness. When the trip was initially given to us, I was unwilling to leave my children. I told my husband I wouldn't go and be on the other side of the world for ten days. I was unwilling to leave my children to spend time with my husband.

Do you hesitate leaving your children to spend time with your husband? Does your husband hesitate leaving your children to spend time with you? Most often, mothers have a harder time leaving their children. But many families find dads forgetting that the marriage needs to come first.

How do we move from being child-centered to marriage-centered? We start by identifying a major misconception: "I could never leave my children, they *need* me. Besides, no one can care for their needs as well as I can."

I believed that. I truly believed the best thing I could do for my children was to meet their every need all the time. I believed that leaving them occasionally would rob them of a stable environment. I believed that no one, not even their dad, could care for their needs as I could.

And my marriage was falling apart in the midst of it all.

Mark and I did go to Italy together and God used that trip—ten days alone with my husband—to teach me the value of my marriage. My children do need me. And quite frankly, I do excel at taking care of their needs; after all, I'm the one who is with them most. But

> What my children need even more than my attention to their every need is my attention to the man I married— their father.

what my children need even more than my attention to their every need is my attention to the man I married— their father. This is truly what will bring stability into their daily lives. When they know Mom loves Dad and Dad loves Mom, their world is in order. That's the beauty of wife first, mother second. Everyone wins. The marriage relationship flourishes and the parenting relationship is enhanced.

I still struggle leaving my kids for any extended length of time. I cry. They cry. But then I have a wonderful time with my husband, and they have a wonderful time with Grandma or whoever is watching them while we're gone. Doing the right thing isn't always easy, but it's right. And the benefits are seen in the years to come.

Our older daughter, Anne, remembers when we rarely invested in our marriage relationship. She now sees us take trips together, go out weekly, and put our relationship first. She also says she would much rather live in our family of today than our family of yesterday. From the mouth of babes is where we learn the most about ourselves.

Personal Reflections

1. Do you struggle with being a wife first and a mother second? List three ways you can make a priority shift by putting your husband first.

❧

2. IDENTIFY three ways you and your husband operate as a team in parenting decisions. Identify two ways you can improve in this strategy.

❧

3. WHAT can you put in place in your relationship to keep the "Who Are You?" question from entering your empty-nest season of marriage?

For Husbands Only

Your wife just read a chapter discussing the importance of being marriage-centered rather than child-centered. This concept is often hard for a woman to grasp. It may be hard for a wife to leave the children with a sitter or a grandparent on occasion. Yet the marital relationship is not meant to operate on autopilot. It needs time away from the children to flourish and grow. The physical relationship is directly affected by the nonsexual time that a husband and wife spend together.

Do you struggle leaving your children in the care of others? Do you find yourself making everything else (work, community organizations, church ...) more important than spending time with your wife? It is not always the wife who finds it difficult to keep the marriage in first place.

Children find stability knowing that Mom and Dad love each other. Mom and Dad's marital relationship defines their world. Commit today to make your marriage first! Be a husband first and a dad second!

Mark

chapter 6

∽

He's Not Wrong—Just Different!

WHEN MARK AND I began to date, we were attracted by
our differences. It only took about six months of marriage
for those same differences to tick us off! In fact, most of us
spend our marriages trying to change our spouse rather
than valuing the way that God created him differently.

I certainly fell into that category. I fell in love with a
man who was a dreamer, a man with a vision. On the
other hand, I married a man who rarely pays attention to
detail. I fell in love with a man who was a coffee connoisseur. On the other hand, I married a man who leaves
coffee spills all over the kitchen floor. Do you see how
one's perspective changes?

Ogden Nash once said, "Marriage is the alliance of two
people, one of whom never remembers birthdays and the
other never forgets them." Often this is the crux of our
frustrations in marriage: differing priorities. We are truly
different from each other, and if we don't appreciate our
differences as being complementary, we'll allow them to
rip us apart.

When Mark and I found ourselves in marriage counseling after hitting rock bottom, we began a new marriage "internship." We really didn't understand marriage,

and we certainly didn't understand each other. During that phase of marriage restoration, I began saying the phrase "He's not wrong; he's just different" many times throughout the day. Mark insists he often heard me saying it under my breath with clenched teeth. The truth is I was shifting my thinking. I began to let go of pride and judgment. Eventually, I came to understand there was more than one way to process decisions, express love, and meet someone else's needs.

Dave Meurer, author of *Daze of Our Wives*, puts it this way, "God has made each one of us to be unique. A great marriage is not when the 'perfect couple' comes together. It is when an imperfect couple learns to enjoy their differences." To get to that point, we need to understand how God has created us differently.[19]

Temperaments

Entire books have been written on personality differences. Quite honestly, I get lost in all the different ways people explain personality types: Are you a golden retriever or an otter? Maybe you are Driven-Intuitive on the DISC scale. How about sanguine or choleric? I have taken many of these tests over the years and I can never remember what any of the words mean!

What is important in understanding personalities is that we are all different. In marriage, we usually find one person who leans toward extroversion and one who is more introverted. We usually find one who is passive and one who is more aggressive. We find one who is a thinker and one who is a feeler. None of these distinctions is right or wrong. They are simply different.

In our home, Mark is the feeler, and I am the thinker. When Mark and I are faced with a decision, I'm the one looking for the facts and all the details. He's processing it based on how he feels. When we were looking for a new home, we would walk into a house and Mark would immediately comment on how it "felt" to him. I, on the other hand, couldn't care less how it felt to me. I wanted to know how many bathrooms it had, the square footage, and whether it had a dishwasher!

Mark's "feeling" comments drove me crazy, and I felt quite alone in my search for the facts while house hunting. But I was missing the gift God gave me in a husband who is different from me. While feelings weren't quite as helpful in finding a home, they are very helpful in relationships.

A person who processes by feeling often possesses discernment and intuition that cannot necessarily be explained. Their "feeling" about a situation may be right, yet they have no evidence to support it. I, as a thinker, take things at face value. I process by facts. If I ask my child a question and he answers it, I am usually satisfied with the answer. My feeling husband, on the other hand, is not always convinced that the simple response was a fully honest answer. He can often sense that something is wrong, when I would completely miss noticing, because I don't have any hard facts to prove it.

Each of us needs to value the way God wired us, differences included. Sometimes facts are needed to make a good decision or to sort out a situation. In those times, Mark has learned to trust my investigative tendencies. At other times, Mark may sense the deeper levels of a situation. When that happens, I have learned to trust his intuitions rather than discount them simply because they lack facts. He and I are made differently, yet our differences—used together—actually make us stronger. We both benefit from the strengths in each other.

You and I have to stop fighting our husbands' differences and begin to celebrate them. We find joy in our relationships when we can honestly say, "Thank you, God, for giving me a husband who has strengths that make my life richer!"

Love Languages

When we were first married, Mark would sometimes stop at the floral shop and buy a bouquet of flowers for me. It was a thoughtful gesture. However, I always felt like it was a waste of our hard-earned money. I didn't want him to buy me things; I just wanted him to spend time with me!

In the same way, on Mark's birthday I would take the day off to be fully available to him by giving him the gift of quality time. Yet he felt disappointed when I didn't give him a purchased birthday gift.

The problem was that Mark and I were speaking different languages to each other. He was speaking "Gift Giving" to me. I was speaking "Quality Time" to him. We were both speaking the language we knew, but not the language the other person would understand as an expression of love.

As we read Gary Chapman's book *The Five Love Languages,* we began to understand how God had made us differently, even in the way we give and receive love. As we've shared Gary Chapman's love languages in our marriage seminars, husbands and wives receive such insight about the unique ways their spouses are wired to give and receive love. See if you can identify yourself in one or two of these languages.

Encouraging Words

A person who "speaks" the language of encouraging words hears "I love you" when someone gives words of encouragement and affirmation. People with this love language find that words mean a lot to them. On the other hand, because words are so important to them, critical words can cause deep hurt.

Acts of Service

In this love language "I love you" is spoken loud and clear when someone does something for another. This is my husband's secondary love language. Because I know that, I can speak love to him by lifting his load sometimes. For instance, we have 2.5 acres we mow each week in the summer. While yard work most often falls under my husband's responsibilities, if I take time to get some or all of the yard mowed before the weekend begins, it is as if I said "I love you! I love you! I love you!" to my husband.

Gift Giving

A special gift, be it large or small, speaks "I love you" to someone whose primary love language is gift giving. The underlying message in this language is "you thought of me while we were apart." This is our teenage son's primary love language. I admit that initially we thought he was very materialistic. When Mark and I would return home from a trip, Evan would immediately ask what we had brought him. After understanding love languages, we began to see that it wasn't the size or kind of gift that was important to him. It was simply the fact that we had thought of him while we were apart.

Quality Time

Some people hear "I love you" when quality, uninter-rupted time and attention is given to them. This is my primary love language. I feel like large deposits accumulate in my love bank when my husband spends undistracted time with me. I'm a stickler for a consistent bedtime for our kids—certainly because they need their sleep—but even more so because I crave quality time with my husband.

Physical Touch and Closeness

A hug, a backrub, holding hands, or just being close is how this love language is communicated. This is my secondary love language. When Mark and I are watching a television show in our family room, I don't want him to be sitting in the recliner while I'm stretched out on the couch. Rather, I want us sitting next to each other, cud-dling on the couch. Quite frankly, I'm in heaven if he's rubbing my back or my feet!

Do you see yourself in any of these expressions of love? Can you identify your spouse's love language based upon what he asks most from you? Are you and your husband speaking two different languages? Make a commitment today to learn a new language—one that speaks love to your husband!

His Needs, Her Needs

He wants sex; she desires affection. He wants affirmation; she wants communication. He desires support from home, while she wants a commitment to family. From the beginning of time, men and women have been frustrated in having their needs met. God says, "the two will become one flesh" (Ephesians 5:31), but how do we make that happen?

Our own selfishness can often keep us from meeting the needs of our spouses. Our self-centeredness deters us from stepping into their world. Yet stepping into their world is exactly what needs to happen in a healthy marriage. Each of us needs to be willing to explore the other's world, becoming more familiar with it everyday. Although I may not have the same needs as my husband, because we are a team I need to value how God has made him. And he may not have the same love languages I do, but he needs to be willing to learn how to step into my world and speak love to me in a way that I understand.

As a result of reading *His Needs, Her Needs* by Willard Harley nine years into our marriage, Mark and I saw that we had wasted many years fighting our differences when we needed to be embracing them. As we better understood the differences in how God created us, we took the risk and explored each other's world. We began to experience more frequent moments of oneness in our marriage. As we changed our approach in meeting one another's needs, we discovered that after spending time learning about the other's world, often stepping into an area we weren't particularly familiar with, we no longer had "his needs" and "her needs," but we now had "our needs." The lines became blurred even in the gender differences as the two of us became one.

So what does Dr. Harley say are the needs of men and women? To further illustrate our differences, here's a peek at his list of ten marriage needs.

She Needs Affection

Affection is defined as nonsexual touch and general expressions of love. (My husband still isn't sure that "non-sexual" and "touch" really go together!) Affection is expressed in words, cards, gifts, hugs, kisses, and courtesies.

He Needs Sexual Fulfillment

John Ortberg, a teaching pastor at Willow Creek Community church, says men like to make love to their wife on every day that begins with a T: Tuesday, Thursday, Today, Tomorrow, Taturday, and Tunday! More often desired by men, the need of sexual fulfillment is not about providing sex for your husband … it's about enjoying it. Sexual fulfillment is not so much about the act of sex, but the attitude toward sex.

She Needs Conversation

Most women need to talk about feelings, plans, and the events of the day. Conversation is best when it's uninterrupted and when undivided attention is given to the communication.

One evening, Mark and I started straightening up our toy room after the kids went to bed. It had been a stressful day. My appearance and countenance screamed exhaustion. As we picked up toys, we started talking about our day, our thoughts, and our feelings. An hour passed without us even realizing it. That's when Mark says he noticed the change in me. That one hour of conversation charged my batteries. The brilliance returned to my eyes. My voice reflected a new energy. My conversation need was met and the results were so drastic, Mark says the memory will stay with him forever.

He Needs Recreational Companionship

This need, most often expressed by husbands, is about keeping the fun in your marriage. Most husbands desire their wives to come out and play with them—to just have fun together.

Early in our marriage, Mark bought us matching bowling balls. Several years later, he asked me to join him in racquetball. In recent years, he has requested that I join him on the golf course. What is it with sports? I've never enjoyed participating in sports at all and quite honestly my husband isn't exactly a sports enthusiast. But after reading Dr. Harley's book, it hit me that it isn't about bowling, or racquetball, or golf at all. It's about recreational companionship. My husband wants us to share some fun together just as we did before we were married. My desire to play golf hasn't changed over the years, but my desire to meet my husband's needs has. Stepping into his world and meeting his need for recreational companionship strengthened the bonds of our marriage in ways I could never have imagined.

She Needs Honesty and Openness

Trust is built in a marriage that is honest and open. This need, which is usually quite high on a woman's list, is about revealing positive and negative feelings, sharing events of the past, discussing plans for the future, and answering questions truthfully. When Mark and I were first married, he withheld information from me about a major purchase of carpet installation tools. The trust that was broken from that one incident took years to mend because my need for honesty and openness was not met.

He Needs an Attractive Spouse

Just in case you haven't figured this one out, men are stimulated by what they see. In Dr. Harley's research, he found that one of a man's top five needs is having an attractive spouse. Before you completely dismiss that as not on the woman's list of needs, you need to know that many women identify this as one of their top needs as well. The gender differences are just a general guideline, certainly not set in stone.

Before you get uptight about feeling like you need to measure up to Cindy Crawford, let me define this need for you in laymen's terms. Being an attractive spouse simply means that you need to look better in the afternoon than you did in the morning when he left you in your bathrobe and slippers! In other words, we need to take care of our bodies and our physical appearance.

I flunked this one when I first stayed home after having children. Sometimes in the late afternoon Mark would find me looking exactly as I did when he left me in the morning—sometimes worse! I wasn't much to look at, and I didn't smell too good either. I definitely was not understanding his need for an attractive spouse.

She Needs a Financial Plan

This isn't about who writes the checks, but rather understanding the family strategy regarding debt, spending, and financial goals and direction. Understanding the financial plan is knowing *how* debt is being handled, *how* the family is meeting financial obligations, and *how* future financial decisions will be made. It is understanding insurance coverage and retirement savings. The need for a financial plan sometimes includes deciding together how to handle financial obligations and challenges, regardless of who actually manages the family's day-to-day finances.

He Needs Support from Home

Support from home is defined as creating a home environment that offers a refuge from the stress and chaos of life. It's also knowing that "home" (spouse and children) supports him as a person in what he is doing in life's venture.

Early in our marriage, I didn't meet this need at all. My critical spirit did not make home a safe place. It was not a refuge from the stress and chaos of life; in fact, Mark did not feel support from home in any way.

She Needs Family Commitment

Knowing that a husband places his family as a higher priority than work, hobbies, or other interests is a need most women view as important. Family commitment is conveyed through time, energy, and emotional availability. Actions speak louder than words.

He Needs Admiration

Most men rank admiration in their top five needs. Admiration is the communication of respect, value, and appreciation. It is rarely critical and expresses value clearly and often. I failed in this as well. My critical spirit and sharp tongue rarely uttered words of encouragement, respect, or value.

We Both Need Spiritual Commitment

After several years of mentoring couples, Mark and I believe we discovered this eleventh need of a healthy marriage. Both men and women who have a relationship with Jesus Christ communicate the desire to share with their spouse a commitment to God and the local church. This need is met when both husband and wife consider themselves on a spiritual journey together.

We Are So Different, Yet We Are the Same

As individuals, we are unique. As men and women, we may have common gender-based differences. Yet, as human beings, we all have the same basic needs: to be loved, accepted, and valued.

Each of us has an "emotional bank." Think in terms of a financial institution, where we make deposits and withdrawals. In marriage, when Spouse A meets the needs of and expresses love to Spouse B, Spouse A is making deposits into the marital account. When needs aren't met or criticism or harsh judgment is spoken, withdrawals are made from the bank. Our goal is to make more deposits than withdrawals.

> *When we make choices that are deposits in our marriage love bank, those investments are sure to pay high relational dividends both inside and outside the bedroom.*

You and I make choices every day. We can choose to love or not to love. We can choose selfishness or selflessness. We can choose to step into our husband's world or stay isolated in our own. When we make choices that are deposits in our marriage love bank, those investments are sure to pay high relational dividends both inside and outside the bedroom.

Personal Reflections

1. IDENTIFY your love language. Which one represents what you request most often from your spouse?

2. NOW identify your husband's love language. What does he request most often from you?

3. STUDY the list of needs in this chapter. Of the eleven needs listed, rank your top five needs. If your husband is willing, have him do the same. Now make a date and compare your lists, discussing how these needs being met fills your emotional love bank.

For Husbands Only

Sometimes I think Jill and I speak completely different languages. We are so different that we used to find ourselves frustrated with one another quite often. However, the frustration has diminished in the past few years as we learned how to appreciate the differences and recognize how we complement each other.

The chapter your wife just read is one you will find very interesting. Take a few minutes and read the love language descriptions on pages 120–21. Can you identify your primary love language? Can you recognize your wife's love language?

Now skip over to pages 123–26 and read the descriptions of the eleven needs of a marriage. Can you pick out your top five needs? They'll probably jump off the page as you connect with them. Take a few minutes to talk about your discoveries with your wife. Listen as she identifies her needs and her love language.

When I began to focus more on Jill and less on myself, our marriage took on a different feel. Intimacy deepened and understanding replaced frustration. Try stepping into her world every once in a while. It may be a little uncomfortable at first, but the benefits outweigh the risks!

Mark

chapter 7

What Are the Messages Only You Hear?

SHARON AND I talked over a cup of coffee about the positive changes happening in her marriage. Scott was making an effort for the first time in their married life. They sought counseling and attended their first marriage retreat. She also learned about how her "controlling" nature had damaged their marriage.

I told Sharon about our marital struggles and particularly about my "take charge" attitude and Mark's passive tendencies. I communicated some of the lessons God had taught me over the years about submitting and following rather than controlling. When I gave her some practical tips to help Scott lead and help her learn to follow, she stated, "These are great ideas. I can't wait to share them with Scott."

However, what she said next was the most important—and telling—part of our conversation. "Jill, I have to be honest with you. Here is what is going on inside my head: *These are great ideas, but why do I always have to be the one who comes up with or hears about the great ideas? Why can't he generate some strategy?*

Here I am pouring my heart out and talking about this, and he's at work and probably hasn't even given me or our marriage one thought today at all!"

I told Sharon that I understood her thoughts about her husband. I had experienced the same condemning, prideful thoughts in my marriage. I also helped her to see the damage that was happening in her marriage by simply entertaining the thoughts in her head.

Have you been there? Can you identify with what she was feeling? Do you have any idea how often your thoughts about your spouse are critical, demeaning, and damaging? Our minds have incredible power in determining our attitudes and our actions. Have you ever taken inventory of your thought life?

Take Your Thoughts Captive

God knows the capabilities of the human mind. He also knows sin always starts in our thoughts. That's why God addresses our thought life multiple times in the Bible. In 2 Corinthians 10:4–5 we read, "The weapons we fight with are not the weapons of the world. On the contrary, they have divine power to demolish strongholds. We demolish arguments and every pretension that sets itself up against the knowledge of God, and *we take captive every thought to make it obedient to Christ*" (italics mine).

There exists a spiritual battle you and I can't see. It's a battle for our marriages. God desires our marriages to last a lifetime. He equips us to achieve that goal. Satan wants our marriages to end. He works very hard to destroy them in any way possible.

There is an enemy, but it is *not* your husband, as much as it might feel that way at times. Satan is a liar and a destroyer (John 8:44). In 1 Peter 5:8, Peter says, "Be self-controlled and alert. Your enemy the devil prowls around like a roaring lion looking for someone to devour."

Leslie Vernick addresses this battle in her book *How to Act Right When Your Spouse Acts Wrong:*

Sometimes [the enemy] uses our spouse to accomplish that purpose, making him or her *feel* like the enemy. That is Satan's plan. His tactics always involve sin, and so we often end up fighting each other instead of fighting our real enemy. When we react sinfully to our spouse's wrongs, Satan wins.[20]

I know the exact point in time our marriage took a turn for the better. It was the day I took an honest inventory of *my* thought life and determined to stop fighting the symptoms and look deep within for the root of the problem. Sure, Mark brought his share of problems into our marriage; in fact, he brought huge problems into our home. Remember the suitcases we talked about in chapter 2? Mark carried about twenty-five suitcases into our marriage; I, on the other hand, seemed to bring in only about five.

With this seemingly uneven share of responsibility for the mess our marriage was in, I became an expert finger pointer. My criticism, both verbally and nonverbally, was killing our marriage. The moment I took responsibility for the damage I was doing, regardless of what Mark brought into the mix, is when I first saw hope for our dying relationship.

Your relationship may not be on the rocks as mine was. Even so, it is important to take an inventory of what messages are being played on mental tapes only you can hear. This is where marriage damage always finds its roots.

Unforgiving Thoughts

Bill Cosby once said, "A good marriage is the union of two good forgivers." I agree. I learned the power of forgiveness over the years.

Forgiveness is a choice. If we wait to forgive until we feel like it, we'll never arrive at our destination. In understanding forgiveness, most of us make the mistake of thinking that it is necessary only in response to big infractions of trust, such as an affair, deceit, or rage. In reality, forgiveness is needed on a daily, hourly, even minute-by-minute basis.

I am human. My husband is human. We will make mistakes. We will disappoint each other. We will cause hurt for the other person by our insensitivities. We will forget to do what we are asked to do. These are the hurts that happen daily in marriage.

Mark tends to leave his shoes out in the middle of the bedroom. He leaves them wherever he happens to be standing when he takes them off. I've asked him many times to please put his shoes in the closet when he's not wearing them. Yet he frequently forgets.

> In understanding forgiveness, most of us make the mistake of thinking that it is necessary only in response to big infractions of trust, such as an affair, deceit, or rage. In reality, forgiveness is needed on a daily, hourly, even minute-by-minute basis.

Each morning, I go into our bedroom to make the bed and tidy things up. I often find his shoes wherever he walked out of them. I pick them up, put them in the closet, *and I forgive him.* It is a conscious thought process that takes place in my head where I say, "God, I forgive Mark for leaving his shoes in the middle of the room." Then I'm done with it. I'm finished. Oh, we might have a conversation about it in the future. In a time of nonconflict, I might kindly ask him to remember to put his shoes away. However, I'll do it with a kind, forgiving heart rather than an angry, I-feel-like-I'm-being-taken-advantage-of attitude. It all comes down to choosing forgiveness.

Forgiveness is closely related to something God calls grace. Grace is unmerited and undeserved favor. I like to think of grace as allowing another person to be human. It is giving someone the space to make mistakes and creating a safe environment of love and forgiveness. God extends grace to us, even though we don't deserve it. He sets the example for us to extend grace to our husbands when they don't deserve it either.

Critical Thoughts

Janine sat at my kitchen island emptying a box of Kleenex. The tears flowed freely as she told me about the lack of both emotional and physical intimacy in her marriage. Janine was an expert at knowing how Jack needed to change. I listened as she carefully laid out her suggestions for improving their relationship. Jack indeed had made some poor choices. He was not everything a husband could be. However, when Janine finished her well-thought-out recipe for marriage restoration, I noticed there were some important ingredients missing from her recipe. Jack's ingredients were identified, but hers were absent.

I gently responded to her thoughts, "Janine, when you think about Jack, do you ever say these kinds of things to yourself: *He is such a fool. Why can't he get it right? What a jerk. How did I manage to marry such an idiot?*"

Janine was caught off guard by what seemed like my ability to read her mind. "How did you know?" she asked.

"Because those are the thoughts I've had in my head about my husband, and I know I'm not alone," I replied. I then shared with Janine how God had helped me to see the plank in my own eye. I explained how he assisted me in recognizing the negative, marriage-destroying thoughts in my head that eventually came to light in my tone of voice or in my attitude toward my husband.

You and I have the ability to build up or destroy the people around us. Our words can be words of life or words of death. But simply treating the symptoms (the words) without looking at the root (the thoughts) will never bring about the needed change of heart.

So how do we begin to "take our thoughts captive"? This was a hard journey for me, and one that I still struggle with sometimes. When tired or angry, I can default here very quickly. Along the way, God showed me very specifically how to inventory my thought life and what to do with the ungodly messages only I can hear. If you struggle with critical thoughts, maybe these can help you as well.

Recognize the Thoughts

If you have had a critical mind-set for years, it takes some time to recognize the lies that are going on in your head. They have found a good home in your thoughts. You've become accustomed to them and can even rationalize why they are true. Begin to notice what thoughts you are entertaining, especially when your husband frustrates or disappoints you. This is the first step in fighting the battle in your mind.

Identify the Enemy

Some years ago I read Frank Peretti's books *This Present Darkness* and *Piercing The Darkness*. Wow! Did those books open my eyes to the spiritual battle around us! Although these books are fiction, they take the spiritual world and personify it in such a way that we can better understand what we cannot see. The Bible talks about both angels and demons at work all around us. When I have critical thoughts in my head, I visualize a demon sitting on my shoulder whispering awful things about Mark into my ear. That's the enemy I need to be fighting!

Replace the Lies with God's Truth

Several years ago, I attended a Neil Anderson ministry seminar based on his book *Victory Over the Darkness*. The seminar featured a list of attributes of who we are in Christ (see Appendix B). After powerfully claiming those for myself, I realized that these truths applied to my husband as well. I used this list each time I needed to replace the enemy's lies about my husband with God's truth.

Forgive and Offer Grace

Forgiveness, as previously discussed, will bring about the much needed closure to the battle in your mind. It is a choice we make to bring God's peace to our heart.

Self-Centered Thoughts

Mark had been irritable for a few days. Nothing big, just impatient and easily irritated with the common things of a life that includes a wife and four children. The first day I offered him grace. We all get bent out of shape sometimes. The second day I asked him what was wrong. He offered little insight. My patience grew thin. By the third day the thoughts going on inside my head went something like this: *What's up with him? Doesn't he know that I need his attention and help? He resents having to be bothered with attending the kids' end-of-the-year school functions. I have to hold his hand in remembering anything that has to do with home. He wants sex, but seems to not pay one bit of attention to me during the day.*

On the fourth day, I noticed a change. There was energy in his voice. He seemed to be back to his old self. He even joked with me when I asked him what brought about the change. He teasingly smiled and told me that he had finally started his period so his PMS was gone.

Mark went on to tell me about the battle he had been fighting the past few days. As the lead pastor in a new church plant, the responsibilities of preaching, counseling, leading staff, and handling administrative details was incredibly overwhelming to him. He faced major direction-setting decisions and felt heavy with the responsibility. He was fighting the urge to run away from it all.

> I made it all about me when it really was all about him. You and I do this all the time. We error on the side of negatively and inaccurately interpreting our husbands' actions.

That's when I realized the error of my ways. I made it all about me when it really was all about him. You and I do this all the time. We error on the side of negatively and inaccurately interpreting our husbands' actions.

Leslie Vernick addresses this as well:

> It is tempting to focus all our attention on how our spouse has hurt or angered us. It is crucial, however, that we begin to understand that our feelings are caused not by our spouse's behavior, but by the way we *interpret* his or her behavior (italics mine).[21]

You and I will most likely make life center on us rather than be concerned about another. It's our human, self-centered nature.

If I had thought more about Mark's needs than my own, I might have interpreted his behavior differently. Can you imagine the difference in the love, grace, and even encouragement I could have given him if I had thought something like this? *Mark doesn't usually act like this. He's carrying a lot of responsibility. I need to lighten his load at home and build him up. Now would be a great time to speak his love language and offer him affirmation.*

Certainly there are times Mark has issues with me and I with him. However, the only way we will make headway in our disagreement is through communicating our disappointments and giving and receiving forgiveness. Falsely interpreting our spouses' actions with self-centered thoughts only leads us in the direction of unnecessary conflict.

A friend once noted that we don't usually see and hear things as they are, but rather as *we* are. We each tend to see life through our own self-centered filter. Leslie Vernick addresses this when she writes,

> We interpret all our spouse's behaviors, labeling each as good or bad, kind or mean, wrong or right. Sometimes our interpretations are inaccurate. Part

of understanding ourselves and growing through our marriage difficulties is to recognize that we interpret all behavior through a lens that colors our understanding of things and to recognize that our lens may not always be telling us the truth.[22]

It is hard to be objective in interpreting our husbands' actions, but it's not impossible. I have learned to say to myself, "It's not about me. This is Mark's stuff." This helps me remain as objective as possible. I may find out later that it was about me, but I'm not responsible for that until it's been communicated to me.

Why is this important to the sexual relationship in a marriage? Quite simply, when it comes to our physical relationship, I'm much more likely to desire physical intimacy if the thoughts in my head are grace giving rather than cluttered with condemnation.

Tempting Thoughts

Dear Jill,

I know you don't know me, but I've heard you teach on the sexual relationship in marriage. I'm a young mom, married seven years to a man who is a good husband and a good father. The problem is that I'm finding myself attracted to another man. I don't know what to do with all my feelings. Can you help me?

Sincerely,

A mom of three

What should we do when tempting thoughts enter our minds? What do we do if the grass looks greener on the other side of the fence? How can we battle the thoughts that justify and rationalize immorality?

Once again, we are addressing an issue that doesn't begin with an action; it begins with a thought. Giving attention to our thought life is so important. The Bible illustrates this in James 1:14–15: "But each one is tempted when, by his own evil desire, he is dragged away and enticed. Then, after desire has conceived, it gives birth to sin; and sin, when it is full-grown, gives birth to death."

Where does desire start? Always in our thoughts! This is why God tells us to take our thoughts captive. Evaluate them. Filter them through his truth.

After four years of marriage, Mark and I moved to Illinois so he could study for the ministry. We had two small children at the time, and we decided it would be best for me to offer day care in our home to help meet our family's financial needs. To make ends meet, I found a night job at a dinner theater. It was a perfect job for me, a former music teacher, as this was the type of theater where the small staff of waiters and waitresses also performed in the shows. With rehearsals, along with working on the weekends, we employees spent a lot of time together.

After several shows, I found myself looking forward to going to work not just because of the performing, but because I liked my dance partner, Mike. I enjoyed our playful banter, our mutual love for music, and even the physical closeness we shared on the stage.

Mark and I were doing little to nurture our relationship at the time, and he was extremely busy with school. We rarely touched affectionately. He didn't have much time or energy for his attention-craving wife who was now getting her attention needs met by someone else.

You see, thoughts entice you before you even realize it. You rationalize and justify your actions based on your feelings. You give more attention to your husband's lacks while the other person's good qualities are on the forefront of your mind.

One day a bit of conscience began to eat away at me. I glimpsed at the road of destruction I was walking on. I knew it wasn't right and that I couldn't continue in this direction without causing great harm to our family. I summoned every bit of courage I had and told Mark about my feelings.

I remember that very long night. Mark was hurt. I was exhausted. We talked about how we had not been available to each other. We cried. Finally, we decided to seek counseling.

Since that time in our marriage, God has given Mark and me the opportunity to mentor other couples that have faced the same challenges. For many, the affair didn't stop before it became physical. However, there is not a single relationship we have seen in which there was no hope for restoration. When God is involved, healing can take place. There is hope.

What do we do when tempting thoughts enter our mind? Here are a few things I learned from our experience.

Turn on the Light!

The moment I told Mark about my feelings, the power of the temptation was considerably less. In John 3:20–21, Jesus confirms this when he says, "Everyone who does evil hates the light, and will not come into the light for fear that his deeds will be exposed. But whoever lives by the truth comes into the light, so that it may be seen plainly that what he has done has been done through God."

Run Toward Your Marriage and Away from the Temptation

First Corinthians 6:18 says very simply, yet very strongly, "Flee from sexual immorality." I decreased my work hours and increased the time Mark and I spent together. We resumed dating in our relationship. Yes, I grieved what I perceived as a loss, but in time I thanked God for what I had gained in my marriage.

Allow for Honest Communication in Your Marriage

I believe one of the reasons we were able to restore our relationship is because Mark *responded* rather than *reacted*. Instead of blowing up in anger, he asked questions and took ownership of his own lack of attention to our relationship. I could be honest because he created an environment in which it felt safe to be honest. While you cannot be assured of your spouse's response to such communication, you can evaluate how you would handle this information if your spouse came to you. Our marriages are more likely to remain intact when we learn how to act right even when our spouses act wrong.

Seek Help

Going to a counselor is not a sign of weakness; it is an act of strength. Knowing when we need to ask for help takes courage. There are resources available to help you invest in your marriage. Take advantage of all that is available to you.

Wrap-Up

You and I are on a journey of character development. As we grow and mature in our faith, God gives us more joy than we could ever imagine. That joy doesn't come from our circumstances; it comes from the way we learn to handle our circumstances.

Do you have a God-perspective when it comes to your marriage? He is the healer, the truth, and the hope we so desperately need every day. Trust him to lead you as you travel on the journey of marriage.

Personal Reflections

1. WHAT are the messages only you hear? Identify as many of them as possible.

2. ASK God to help you recognize these thoughts when they surface in your mind. When you identify negative, condemning thoughts about your husband, replace them with God's truth (see Appendix B).

⌐◦⌐

3. IDENTIFY one time in the last week when you saw a situation through a self-centered lens. Ask God to forgive you for your insensitivity to the other person.

For Husbands Only

Have you ever had an argument with your wife in your head when she didn't have a clue you were angry with her? I have! I learned, however, that the condemning, judgmental thoughts in my head cause damage to my marriage even if I never say them aloud to my wife.

This chapter challenged your wife to evaluate her thought life—something every married person should do. Critical, condemning thoughts come across in our tone of voice or the heavy sigh of frustration. Tempting thoughts lure us to believe that the grass is greener on the other side of the fence. Unforgiving thoughts keep us stirred up about even the smallest human error. Self-centered thoughts make every disagreement about *us* and blind us to the struggles others have.

God wants us to know there is a battle for our marriages. It's a spiritual battle we cannot see. There is an enemy—and it is not your wife (regardless of how it feels in times of disagreement!). Satan wants to steal your joy and ruin your marriage. If you and I don't identify the thoughts that erode our love relationship and put them to death, we will never experience the love relationship God designed in marriage.

Regrettable actions begin with ungodly thoughts. Capture the thoughts today before they become the hurts of tomorrow.

Mark

chapter 8

Make the Marriage Investment

As an insurance agent, Tim took multiple classes that included tests. Once a year he attended a seminar that brought him up to date on the changing laws of insurance. It was an important part of his continuing education.

Teri started her home party business when her youngest child began school. She felt it would give the family a second income while allowing her to use her people skills. As a member of the sales force for this company, Teri attended a monthly regional meeting and an annual sales conference. Teri saw these opportunities as continuing education for her business investment.

James had always wanted to be a teacher. After graduating from college, he found a teaching job in a small school district near his hometown. To renew his teaching certificate, James had to take nine hours of continuing education classes every two years. These classes kept him on the cutting edge of his profession and equipped him with new skills to use in the classroom.

There are 168 hours in every week. The average married person in the paid workforce spends 40–50 hours per week at his or her job. The other 118–28 hours are spent at home directly or indirectly interacting with spouse.

In the workforce, we rarely question the continuing education investment required by many companies to meet professional standards. But when such an investment is suggested for marriage, the excuses abound. In the very place we spend almost 75 percent of our time— our marriage—we have little or no education, and we do nothing to invest in the relationship. What's wrong with this picture?

> *In the very place we spend almost 75 percent of our time—our marriage—we have little or no education, and we do nothing to invest in the relationship. What's wrong with this picture?*

We meet the man of our dreams, fall in love, get married, and then find ourselves frustrated with him and he with us. We believe the problem lies with him; however, the problem usually lies in the fact that *most of us don't know how to be married*. Instead of discovering how we can complement each other, we strive to change the other person to be more like us. Instead of looking for resolution in conflict, we are driven to win the argument even at the expense of our spouse's feelings or self-esteem. Instead of planning time together without the children, we find every excuse in the book why we can't be alone together, and then wonder why our marriage is falling apart.

Marriage education usually takes place in the home in which we grew up and the movies we have watched. Some of us watched our parents model good marital skills. On the other hand, with a divorce rate of about 50 percent, many of us were obviously not so lucky.

Rob Marus notes in a *Christianity Today* article how little he as a teen learned about marriage from his church: "My youth minister never said anything about how difficult marriage might be after we found that special someone. I can't blame him; he was too busy making sure that we would defer sex until marriage to tell us much about what came afterward."[23]

If you have learned about marriage from the media, let's consider that a substandard education. Maybe you had a few sessions of premarital counseling. That's a great start, but it's only the beginning. Once you are knee-deep in the marriage relationship, you'll find it a lot harder than you expected.

Most couples that come to us for mentoring make the comment that marriage shouldn't be this hard and that maybe they weren't made for each other. This is incorrect thinking. Marriage *is* hard work and they *are* made for each other. We just have to learn how to be married and learn skills that will help our marriages succeed.

Where do we find marriage training? There are many types of continuing-education opportunities available.

Seminars and Retreats

Beth and Brad elbowed one another all evening. As the husband and wife team taught the Friday evening session at the marriage seminar, Beth and Brad thought that hidden cameras had been placed in their home as the presenters addressed the very things they struggled with in their marriage. The seminar leaders discussed the differing needs of a husband and wife, and Beth and Brad related to almost everything they said. At the end of the evening, Brad confessed his reluctance to attend the two hour seminar; he had gone just to make Beth happy. He now saw how valuable the seminar was to understanding himself and understanding his wife. He was pleased to be learning some skills to help take their marriage to a deeper level.

Most of us wrongly believe that marriage seminars and retreats are for couples with marital troubles. While many struggling marriages have been saved at seminars and retreats, most are designed to be preventative health care for healthy marriages.

Fear of the unknown most often keeps people from attending a marriage seminar. Often husbands ask if they will have to speak in front of the group for any reason. The answer is probably not—and definitely not if they don't want to. Most marriage seminars and retreats are designed as classroom settings in which participants learn and discuss with their spouses how the information applies to their personal relationship. Good seminar leaders use a lot of personal stories along with large doses of humor to create a fun, lighthearted, yet instructive atmosphere.

In central Illinois, Mark and I teach a seminar known as the ABC's of a Healthy Marriage every spring and fall. Here is a sampling of some of the comments we received after one of our recent seminars:

"My wife dragged me here almost against my will—but I'm so glad she did. This was the best seminar I've ever attended. I can't believe how much I've learned!"

"I have learned so much about myself and my husband—I know this will make our good marriage even better."

"Before coming, we were ready to call it quits. Now we realize that we really don't know how to be married. We're ready to work harder, get the help we need, and make this marriage work."

I've never talked to anyone who has felt that a marriage seminar was a waste of time. People may have hesitated to come in the beginning, but by the end they are wondering how they could have ever missed it.

Published Resources

Bookstore shelves are increasingly stocked with marriage resources. You and I should take advantage of the excellent resources available to us. My friend Julie committed herself to reading one marriage book each year.

She says this keeps her mindful of her marriage priority and sharpens her skills as a wife.

Mark and I find that our reading and discussing of a particular marriage book spurs some great conversation. We read the chapters separately, I with a pink highlighter in hand and he with a blue highlighter. Then we talk about the highlighted parts of the chapter, gaining new perspectives that deepen our bond.

Another good resource is *Marriage Partnership* magazine, a quarterly publication that Mark and I find relevant and encouraging in our journey to experience God's best in our relationship.

There are hundreds of websites available to encourage you in your marriage and connect you to other resources. Check out the appendix at the back of the book for a comprehensive listing of quality marriage resources.

Church

The church is an important educational part of the community. If you are not currently attending church, make it a priority for your family.

Many Sunday school classes and small in-home groups study and discuss the marriage relationship. Marriage seminars and retreats are often church-sponsored events, so you are more likely to find out about these opportunities by being connected with a church.

The church also is where we are reminded of God's love and his desire for us to grow in our character. When we learn more about God, we're more likely to want to make the necessary changes to become the spouse we need to be.

Counseling

Seeking wise counsel is not a sign of weakness; it is a sign of strength, and it's biblically supported! Proverbs 15:22 says, "Plans fail for lack of counsel, but with many advisers they succeed." If struggles become destructive to your relationship, get the help that will lead you toward restoration.

For Mark and me, counseling played a huge role in finding healing in our marriage. The regular appointments with the counselor provided the discipline and structured environment we needed to make changes. Occasionally, we met individually with the counselor to work through issues of our own, but most of the time we both went to the sessions. Early on, when things were difficult, we both arrived with a written agenda of what we wanted to discuss. Most often the list covered things the other person was doing wrong. Over time our lists became shorter, the atmosphere calmer, and our attitudes changed from critical to teachable.

How do you find a good counselor? One place to start is the American Association of Christian Counselors (www.aacc.net). Their online directory can connect you with a counselor in your area. If there is no one from your area in the directory, check out the yellow pages and look specifically for a Christian counselor.

How important is it to have a counselor that is a Christian? I say very important. The world offers us relative truth. God gives us *absolute* truth. There is right and there is wrong. When it comes to sorting out confusion in a relationship, we need to be able to base our standards on absolute, unchanging standards. With God as the architect of marriage, we also need to consult his original plans (the Bible) for direction in our lives and our marriage.

Mark and I found that interviewing a counselor was very helpful. We also looked around until we found the right fit for both of us. Here are some questions to ask a potential counselor:

- What is your approach to counseling?
- Will you interact with me and give me direction?
- Are you a Christian? If so, is that incorporated in your counseling?

- Are you under supervision or accountability yourself?
- What kind of training and experience do you have in working with my specific problem?
- How many problems like mine have you worked with in the past year?
- Are you the right person to help me make the changes I need, or do you recommend someone else?

All counselors should give you five or ten minutes for an initial phone interview. If someone is bothered by your questions, you should choose someone else. You want to feel comfortable with this new relationship.

What about the cost? Yes, counseling is a financial expense, but your marriage is worth it. You can usually inquire about the fee structure from the receptionist or office manager. You can also inquire about insurance coverage, sliding fees, and payment arrangements. Many medical insurance companies offer coverage for counseling services, often with a limit on the number of visits per year and a required co-pay. Some counselors offer sliding fees based upon income level. It took Mark and me a year to pay off our counseling expenses when we had no appropriate insurance coverage. Yes, it was a financial investment, but one that paid wonderful dividends.

Counseling is also an investment of time. Remember, your problems have been a long time in the making and significant changes won't happen overnight. However, when you look at the big picture of a lifelong, happy marriage, what's a few months or a year of counseling? It's really just a blip on the screen of a fifty-year marriage!

A Good Investment

When we make an investment in the stock market, we choose to set aside a predetermined amount of money to purchase a certain stock. A good return on our money is the goal. This deliberate investment is an important part of a financial strategy.

Our marriage needs the same type of strategic investment. When we set aside time and money to make stock purchases in our marriage, we are on our way to finding an excellent return on our investment. When we strategically plan for continuing educational opportunities, we are doing our best to give our relationship every opportunity to succeed!

Personal Reflections

1. IDENTIFY two educational opportunities you will pursue in the next twelve months. Make a to-do list to help you work toward the goal and make it happen.

2. CHECK out www.familylife.com to find the closest location for an "I Still Do" conference or a Family Life Marriage conference. Discuss with your spouse the possibility of attending.

For Husbands Only

Do you realize that you and I spend only 25 percent of our time at work and 75 percent of our time at home in relationship with our family? We're quick to invest in our careers by attending classes, seminars, or conventions when necessary, but when our wives mention going to a marriage seminar, we scoff at the suggestion.

Have you ever considered whether you and your wife really know how to be married? Do you have the tools that will give your marriage longevity? Are your conflict resolution skills honoring to each other? Do you really understand the differing needs that men and women have? I don't believe any of us knows instinctively how to be married. Our culture operates with the assumption that the moment you utter the words "I do," you immediately know how to have a successful marriage.

In the same way we invest in our careers, we need to invest in our marriages. Marriage seminars and retreats are usually high energy, fun gatherings that spark communication and deepen intimacy between a husband and wife. Attending church together gives a common foundation to a family and connects you to other couples working hard at marriage.

In the difficult times, seeking out a professional counselor can make the difference in a marriage's death or survival. For Jill and me, counseling proved to be invaluable to our relationship. We needed help sorting through the baggage we had carried into our marriage and finding out how to solve the all-too-frequent conflict between us.

Don't make the mistake of being unwilling to invest in your marriage relationship. Put some time, money, and energy into the place you spend 75 perecent of your time. Check out some of the marriage retreats listed in the appendix of this book and kidnap your wife for a weekend away! It's an investment that promises to pay excellent dividends!

Mark

part 4

The Practical Tools—Inside the Bedroom

chapter 9

Sexual Differences: Don't Be Frustrated, Be Fascinated!

As WOMEN, you and I can be standing in a line for the bathroom in a public place, and by the time we reach the stall we may have chatted with the woman in front or behind us. We know a little about her, and she probably knows a little about us. We might even continue the conversation once we're enthroned!

According to my husband, men don't talk in the bathroom. Conversation is taboo, *especially* while "doing their business." Mark and I discussed this one day after I told him about a restroom conversation I'd had. He exclaimed in surprise, "You talked to each other in there? You actually talked between stalls?"

We are different creatures, aren't we? God created us emotionally and physically different. Yet our differences are designed to be complementary. Physically, the male and female bodies fit together like a lock and key. And our approach to the sexual relationship differs in other ways. In *The Mystery of Marriage*, Mike Mason notes,

> When people forget that the opposite sex is oppo-
> site, it can result in men actually resenting women

for not being men, and vice versa. Ultimately this is just one aspect of the way in which people are continually being hoodwinked into assuming they are in relationship with one another, when really all they are relating to is themselves.[24]

Our goal is not to be frustrated with those differences, but to be fascinated by them. To appreciate our differences, we need to understand them fully. In discussing differences, we have to remember that these are generalities. There are certainly exceptions to the rule. However, it is helpful to look at the general differences most often found between men and women. Let's see what we can discover that will help us celebrate our sexual differences.

Approach

For men sex is very physical. In addition to the physical release, the physical exertion of making love is important. For women, sex is very relational. It's about connecting and feeling close. This is why a woman struggles having sex shortly after a marital spat, while a husband wouldn't give it a second thought.

Men tend to be compartmentalized and difficult to distract. They think about one thing at a time, giving it their full focus. Women tend to be wholistic and easily distracted, taking the whole environment into consideration. They think about many things at a time. Let's apply this to a home with children. You're in a moment of physical passion when you hear the pitter-patter of little feet coming down the hallway. You immediately ask, "Is that the kids?" He responds, "What kids? Do we have kids?"

Might there be a reason for this difference? Husbands are providers—designed to go to work, focus on the job, do well for the benefit of the family. Wives are designed to be the nurturers—sensing the needs of others and keeping our eyes on the general well-being of our family. Don't be frustrated; be fascinated!

Men tend to desire variety in the sexual relationship. Women desire security. He's thinking, *Let's do something different—add a little spice to our life.* She's thinking, *I need to know that I can trust him, that our relationship is secure. Don't throw me too many curves or I might feel insecure.* Our husbands need to understand our need for security. At the same time, we have to value our husbands' desire for variety. This may mean we have to creep out of our comfort zone one step at a time.

Most men consider sex a high priority, while most women feel it is a low priority. In his book *His Needs, Her Needs,* Dr. Willard Harley reports that sexual fulfillment is usually on a man's list of top five needs in a marriage, while most women rank sexual fulfillment low on their list of the ten marital needs.[25] God knew what he was doing when he created us to balance each other out. If we both had a high priority for sex, we'd never get anything else accomplished. If we both had a low priority for sex, we'd never have a family! Don't be frustrated by the differences ... be fascinated!

Excitement

Men are stimulated by *sight,* while women are stimulated by *attitudes and actions.* The first time I heard this I told my husband, "See honey, emptying the dishwasher is a form of foreplay!"

Many moms report that when their husbands help with the kids, read the children stories at night, and assist in the kitchen, the women feel physically excited. Even if they don't identify sexual stimulation, they report feelings of closeness, value, and being cared for. These are stepping-stones to physical intimacy.

You probably seldom notice when your husband gets out of the shower, but he usually responds when you do. While loving, serving attitudes and helping, caring actions draw us near to our husbands, what he sees and even smells can stimulate him. A whiff of your perfume, a glimpse of you getting dressed, an outfit he loves for you to wear—these fan the flames of excitement for him.

Your husband's excitement is *immediate* while yours is *gradual*. Have you ever gone away for the weekend and found that he wants to make love as soon as you get to the hotel, while you just want to unwind, reconnect, or go sightseeing? This is because he's wired for a quicker excitement than you are. He's focused on the sexual encounter, while you are more focused on the relational time together.

Sexual Desire and Response

Women tend to be cyclical in their sexual desire. Women's bodies are created with reproduction in mind. This means most women experience a higher desire when they are ovulating. Our fluctuating hormones affect desire.

For most men, it's "any time, any place!" Until age forty, the testosterone level stays steady for him, creating a fairly consistent desire. However, after age forty, the testosterone does begin to drop. Of course, life circumstances, past experiences, children, health issues, medication, age, and stress all affect natural desire for both the husband and the wife.[26]

Women are "consistently inconsistent" according to Dr. Rosenau. One day she may like her breasts stimulated, and at another time she won't want that at all. Men, however, are usually *consistent* in the stimulation they desire. "[They] are very predictable. If you appeal to him visually or rub his penis, he gets excited."[27]

When it comes to a sexual response, men experience quick excitement while women have to warm up slowly. Gary Smalley describes this by saying men are microwaves and women are crock-pots! Furthermore, a study by Masters and Johnson found men can reach a climax in two minutes, while women average eleven minutes. Rather than finding this frustrating, let the differences fascinate you. Marvel in his desire and excitement, allowing it to become contagious. Bask in his yearning for you.[28]

For men, orgasm is usually needed for sexual satisfaction. Men experience shorter and more intense orgasms than women, whose may be longer. Whereas men usually experience a *single* orgasm, women are capable of experiencing *multiple* orgasms.

Having said that, women can sometimes feel satisfied without a sexual release.

Choosing to Make Love

Contrary to culture's definition, love is not a feeling. It is a choice. We choose to love or not to love. Similarly, for women, making love is a choice. Our husbands often desire sex as a hormonal and physical urge; we will more likely willfully choose to make love.

We will also choose to bring pleasure. We will choose to make time for our husbands. We will choose to make the marital relationship the foundation of our families. We will choose to find healing from our pasts. We will choose to take our thoughts captive. Ultimately, we can choose to be frustrated or choose to be fascinated by the ways our husbands are different from us.

Celebrate those differences and enjoy the variety they bring to your lovemaking!

Personal Reflections

1. Can you name two ways your husband sexually responds differently than you do? How can you move from frustration to fascination? Change your attitude? Exhibit more patience? Learn more about him?

2. Identify one difference that always seems to separate the two of you. How can you begin to

see this difference as a complement rather than a complaint?

For Husbands Only

This short chapter provides a quick overview of the way men and women differ sexually. Take five minutes and read the chapter yourself.

Do you respond to the differences with frustration? If so, can you move to find a bit of mystery and fascination in the differences?

Jill and I have always found ourselves at opposite ends of the sexual spectrum. For years we allowed that to divide us. However, we now understand and appreciate how God made us differently to bring a balance to our marriage. We're fascinated by our unique personalities and preferences.

Replace your frustration with fascination as you discover how God has designed you to fit together perfectly in marriage.

Mark

chapter 10

Let Me Please You: Understanding the Concept of "Pleasuring"

IT TOOK ME almost twenty years of marriage to begin to understand that sex is a gift of pleasure. God wants us to enjoy our bodies, and he created us to be sexual beings. Just as a full meal brings satisfaction to our hunger, an enjoyable, loving sexual relationship satisfies our desire for love, touch, and intimacy in marriage.

Can a woman be a Christian and still be sensual? Absolutely! Is *sensual* a word used in marriage? You bet! God wants you and me to delight in our sexuality and to fully enjoy the physical union of our marriage.

How do we do that? We focus on the fine art of pleasuring.

It's More Than Just Sexual Intercourse

Bringing sexual pleasure to each other is a learned skill that improves throughout the life of a marriage. It is a journey of exploration—together—that leads to deeper intimacy, more fun, and increased pleasure.

When we change our focus from making intercourse our destination to making pleasure our goal, an exciting experience of sexual love awaits us! Dr. Rosenau puts it this way, "Sex in marriage has an ever-changing, renewing quality to it.... A routine sex life is not God's design. You can make love four times a week for the next fifty years and still never plumb the surprising depths of this mysterious sexual 'stream' of becoming one flesh."[30]

> *When we change our focus from making intercourse our destination to making pleasure our goal, an exciting experience of sexual love awaits us!*

Pleasuring is when both husband and wife are excited about bringing physical delight to each other. Imagine a conversation where he begins with, "Let me please you," followed by her response, "No, no, let me please you!" Pleasuring can be a give-and-take of irresistible fun.

How do we move beyond simple intercourse to explore the fine art of pleasuring? There is a two-part answer to that question: We have to know how to *give* pleasure, and we have to learn how to *receive* pleasure.

Giving Pleasure

In *A Celebration of Sex*, Dr. Rosenau talks about becoming a sexual connoisseur. What a wonderful term as we learn about giving pleasure! When we marry, our culture tells us to expect good sex right away. Truth be known, most of us really don't know how to give pleasure. All too often we get into lovemaking ruts; we rush through sex; we stay in old habits because we don't know how to expand our experiences.

Although this book is not a clinical book on sexual technique, my hope is to give you suggestions and additional resources to expand your thinking about sexual intimacy. This discussion is the result of my own journey from viewing sex as an obligation to realizing the unending playground of pleasure God designed for us.

We need to begin by learning about the way a man's body works. Start by identifying his erogenous zones. Explore these areas with different kinds of touch, pressure, and stimulation to give him pleasure. Be a student of your husband, learning every square inch of his body— remembering what excites him without being stuck in boring patterns of stimulation. Dr. Rosenau divides the body into three levels of erogenous zones:

Level 3: The skin is the most extensive area of sensuality. Pleasure your mate's skin by touching, massaging, and caressing. Although arms, shoulders, scalp, upper chest, buttocks, and calves may not have the concentration of nerve endings as other parts of the body, they are still very sensual.

Level 2: The inner thighs, breast area, abdomen, navel, small of the back, the palms of the hands, the neck, and the face including the eyelids, temples, mouth, and tongue are parts of the body rich with sensory nerve endings. Explore these with fingertips, mouth, and tongue.

Level 1: The most stimulating erogenous zones are the nipples and the genitals. The nipples are sensitive to touch and create pleasurable feelings when stimulated orally or manually. For him, the penis is an intricate network of blood vessels and nerves. The skin on the penis is loosely attached to allow for easy stimulation. If you are unsure how to give pleasure to his penis, ask your husband to demonstrate or communicate to you the strokes or touches he prefers in sexual pleasure. For you, the nipples and clitoris bring the most sexual satisfaction.[30]

Our bodies are designed to progress from Level 3 to Level 2 and then to Level 1. Women find it especially difficult to go straight to Level 1. In fact, it's almost physically impossible. Men, however, can often start at Level 2 or 1. Communication is the key to knowing what your spouse desires, at what level to begin, and when to move to the next level each time you make love.

Be creative, gentle, loving, and giving. Drive him crazy with the pleasure you offer. Use your hair, your tongue, and your skin to tantalize the nerve endings all over his body. Increase your intimacy by studying your husband and his sexual likes and dislikes. Develop your ability to give pleasure by exploring and experimenting with what feels most exciting and pleasurable to him.

Receiving Pleasure

God created you to enjoy feelings of sexual arousal as well. He gave you the ability to experience and enjoy pleasurable feelings. He designed your body to receive sexual pleasure.

Did you know that God gave you, as a woman, a part of your body that has no other purpose than sexual pleasure? While doing research for this book, I ran across this statement by Dr. Rosenau, "The clitoris is given to the female solely for sexual pleasure."[32] I reread this over and over—struck by its significance. Do you realize how important this is to understanding God's design for sex, feeling comfortable with our sexuality, and moving past inhibitions? We need to know that God created a part of our bodies *exclusively* for sexual pleasure. That little sentence says a lot!

God intended men to experience the highest level of sexual satisfaction from stimulation of the penis. However, the penis has several different functions. In contrast, the only function of a woman's clitoris is sexual pleasure. It's not even necessary for human reproduction. Imagine how much he wants us to enjoy this gift. His goal of allowing us to feel pleasure and satisfaction is so evident when we understand this.

Clifford and Joyce Penner put it this way: "The fact that the clitoris in the woman is unique in its function of receiving sexual stimuli ... is confirmation that God intended women to be intensely sexual beings, not just 'vaginas' as recipients of the man's sexual expression."[32]

If you think that sex is just for your husband, think again. Although men possess higher levels of testosterone, which is associated with a higher sex drive, you and I possess a clitoris designed only for sexual pleasure. God designed us differently, but our differences complement each other.

The clitoris needs to be stimulated in order for a woman to reach a sexual climax. I once heard a speaker state that, for a woman, sexual intercourse without clitoral stimulation is like stimulating only a man's testicles, expecting him to come to a climax. It just doesn't work that way.

Remember, all of us learn to be good lovers over many years of marriage. Start by instructing your husband on what feels good to you. Think about the different areas to stimulate in Level 3, Level 2, and Level 1. Where do you need to start? Sometimes the starting point of touch varies depending on the day, the season of life, or the circumstances surrounding the time set aside for intimacy. For instance, a nursing mother may not desire to have her breasts touched when she is engorged with milk.

It is also important for both of you to know that what turns you on physically today might vary tomorrow. That's perfectly normal! Tell him when pressure is too hard or too soft. Inform him if you don't like his tongue in your ear. Guide his hand or his mouth to areas you prefer to be stimulated.

Don't be afraid to respond to pleasure with sounds of satisfaction. Remember, God gave you this gift and desires for you to enjoy it. Groan, breathe loudly, exclaim in excitement, purr with pleasure, squeal with delight, and allow your nonverbal communication to be truly expressive. Your sounds of pleasure excite your husband.[33]

The Phases of Desire and Excitement

There are four phases of desire and excitement in sexual pleasure. To fully understand the steps of desire and excitement, we need a foundation of knowledge.

Phase 1: Arousal begins long before your lovemaking. According to Dr. Ed Wheat, "Every meaningful, fully enjoyable sex act really begins with a loving, attentive attitude hours or even days before." The title of Dr. Kevin Leman's book *Sex Begins in the Kitchen* illustrates this further. Phase 1 ends with foreplay, which is what builds the physical excitement. In other words, this phase begins with emotional excitement and ends in physical excitement.

Phase 2: Sometimes called the plateau phase, Phase 2 is usually the longest and perhaps the most enjoyable of the sexual phases. It is a sensual celebration filled with love play. This stage includes direct stimulation of the erogenous zones and active intercourse. Dr. Rosenau encourages "the wise couple [to intersperse] intercourse throughout the plateau phase as the husband starts and stops and keeps his arousal on a plateau without peaking too soon." This brings a balance to his "microwave" sexual excitement and her "crock-pot" timing needed for physical pleasure.[34]

Phase 3: With increased excitement from the plateau phase, both husband and wife are ready to "climb the last peak with focused stimulation." This is the orgasm phase, allowing the sexual excitement to reach its climax when sexual tension is released.[35]

This phase can be slightly different for men and women. God gave us women something else that he didn't give to men: the ability to have multiple orgasms. Where men need time to recuperate sexually after an orgasm, women don't. In fact, women are capable of having multiple orgasms, often in rapid succession or minutes apart. What great sexual gifts God gave us as women!

Phase 4: The relaxation or resolution phase is a tender time for loving, nonsexual touch including loving gentle caresses, warm cuddling, and gentle kisses. It's a time of affirmation of your love for each other.

Understanding More about Orgasms

As Janine and I drove to the outlet mall, we talked about our marriages. We shared the stories of how we met our husbands, what our weddings were like, and how marriage caused us both to grow in ways we never would have imagined. Eventually, we found ourselves on the topic of sex. Janine blurted out, "Jill, I've never had an orgasm. What is wrong with me?"

"There's nothing wrong with you," I responded. We talked about her lack of interest in sex correlating directly to her inability to reach orgasm.

One of the differences between men and women is that men physically need the release of an orgasm to feel sexually satisfied. On occasion, women can feel sexually satisfied without reaching a climax.

However, "rarely does a woman keep interested in sex if she is not orgasmic," says Joyce Penner in *Marriage Partnership* magazine. An orgasmic release of the sexual tension built up during pleasuring leaves one feeling more relaxed and satisfied.[36]

An orgasmic response in women is primarily related to clitoral stimulation. Some researchers believe there is no such thing as a "vaginal orgasm." Even when climax is attained during intercourse, the clitoris is being stimulated by the position of the penis.

Understanding the sexual techniques of pleasuring can make a huge difference in finding sexual satisfaction and reaching orgasm. Remember, God gave women the clitoris for no other reason. You and your husband need to learn how to use what God has given you. If you are looking for an excellent, Christian book on sexual technique, one of the best is Dr. Douglas Rosenau's book *In Celebration of Sex*.

Where Do I Start If I've Never Had an Orgasm?

God designed our bodies to respond sexually, and having sex only to satisfy your husband will eventually cause you to lose interest in sex. The sexual relationship was created to be a mutually satisfying experience.

What if you have tried and tried and still had no success? Joyce Penner addresses this in her article entitled "What Every Woman Needs To Know About Sexual Satisfaction." She first says to stop trying and instead work toward releasing responsiveness. In doing so, here are some steps to take:

1. *Obtain a medical evaluation.* If something is wrong physically, all the efforts in the world will never produce an orgasm. Ask the doctor to start with a hormonal evaluation checking estrogen, progesterone, and testosterone levels. If you are on a birth-control pill, inquire about the effects it could have on hormone levels or lubrication during sex.

    In interviewing Dr. Mark Gentry, OB/GYN, he mentioned that the increased use of anti-depressant prescriptions is causing a portion of our population to have a decreased sexual desire. We often forget that the medicine we take will affect our bodies in other ways. At the same time he also mentioned that most often

he finds sexual difficulties emotional and relational in nature, rather than medical in nature.

2. *Pursue self-discovery.* Learn to know your body
   and what feels good to you. Joyce Penner offers
   direction in exploring a genital self-exam in her
   book *Restoring the Pleasure.*

3. *Tune into your body's sexual messages.* Listen
   during the day, listen in the shower, listen during
   sex. Pay attention to even your most subtle
   sexual cues.

4. *Initiate on occasion.* Responsiveness happens
   most often when a woman leads with her sexuality rather than when she succumbs to pressure
   from her husband. This is because a turned-on
   woman is usually a turn-on to a man, but a
   turned-on man can be a pressure to a woman.

5. *Make pleasure your goal.* Focus on the sensa-
   tions of where you are being touched or on
   bringing pleasure to your husband. Make pleasure your goal and allow release and responsiveness to be a natural culmination to pleasure.

6. *Be deliberate about sex.* Planning for times of
   physical connection is important, especially in
   the childrearing years. Spontaneity is wonderful
   when it happens, but if you are looking to
   increase your responsiveness, you need plenty
   of opportunities to explore, connect, cuddle, and
   play together. Plan for those times together.

7. *Kiss passionately every day.* This keeps the pilot
   light on so you can more easily turn up the
   flame. The Penners suggest fifteen minutes a day
   of face-to-face intimacy—sharing emotionally—
   that ends in thirty seconds of passionate kissing
   that does not lead to sex. Women sometimes stop

kissing passionately because they fear it will lead to sex when they don't always want to go there.

8. *Have fun and play together.* Focus on what is working rather than on what isn't. Be creative and experimental in your approach to your physical relationship. As you enjoy the marital playground of sexual intimacy, you're on your way to increasing responsiveness.[37]

What about the Mess of Sex?

God created our bodies to respond to sexual excitement with secretions that provide lubrication for increased pleasure and also make it comfortable for our bodies to be intertwined in intercourse. The secretions are not dirty, but they can be messy. For some, the secretions are a turn-off; for others, a turn-on. Regardless of how you feel about them, they are a reality when making love.

Some couples choose to keep a washcloth or towel close by. Others have their own special love-making sheet or blanket they use. Still others feel no need to take care of the discharge if they make love in bed. They are comfortable letting the sheets absorb it. Sometimes a couple may continue their intimacy after intercourse by showering together. Women often complain of fluid seepage following intercourse and many choose to put on a panty liner or a light feminine pad.[38]

What about Sex During Menstruation?

While there is no physical reason to refrain from sex during menstruation, there are some practical reasons you might choose to refrain during the heavy flow days. This falls under that area of personal preference and is a decision a husband and wife need to make together.

Couples who choose to make love during her period usually find the need to use a towel, sheet, or special love-making blanket to protect bedding from the blood that may leak. Clean up is usually a necessity as well.

When It Comes to Pleasure, Is Oral Sex Okay?

Every book I read in preparation for writing this book addresses this question; obviously it's a question often asked. The Bible does not identify different types of sex within the marriage relationship.

I see the phrase *oral sex* as a cultural term that does us a disservice by damaging God's beautiful plan. Our culture likes to separate sexual activity into different parts to legitimize sexual relations outside of marriage that don't include intercourse. This skewed approach is convenient for people who want to maintain a technical virginity while being sexually active.

The terminology not only isolates certain sexual "acts" from intercourse, but also reduces them to a "sex act" rather than the entire pleasurable, intimate experience that God intended a husband and wife to experience in marriage. Is there really such a thing as "oral sex"? I don't believe so at all. If a husband and wife determine to include oral stimulation in giving and receiving sexual pleasure, they are free to do so. This falls under the area of personal likes and dislikes. It's a part of exploring and experimenting.

But it is important to remember that it is never acceptable for a husband or wife to demand an experience from a spouse if he or she does not enjoy it or is uncomfortable with it. The marital, sexual relationship is a love relationship that includes respect and honor for the other person.

Are "Quickies" Okay?

Some people think of quickies as quick sex when you both are interested, but don't have much time. Other people think of it as a gift one partner might give to the other. While satisfying, marital sex cannot thrive on quickies, there is a time and a place that these expressions of love are appropriate.

If there's not much time, but desire for both parties, a quickie can add a little bit of adventure to your love life. Sometimes it's the unique location that adds to the excitement (a small bathroom for example). Other times it's a "beat the clock" challenge that adds some spice to your life (fifteen minutes before the kids come home).

There are seasons of life when intercourse is not possible or desired. During these times you can remain sexually intimate by giving pleasure to one another. These times might include the final weeks of pregnancy or the six weeks following the birth of a child. Maybe it is when one of you is too tired or recovering from an illness. It could also be when stress relief is needed or when you are working to balance your differing sex drives.

Sexual intimacy does not always involve intercourse; however, a mutually satisfying relationship will need both the adventure of quickies and the enjoyment of lengthy love-making sessions.

Is It Okay to Touch Myself?

God is silent on so many areas—these, I believe, are what he leaves to personal preference and your own journey to seek his will for you. God created your body and wants you to fully experience the pleasure he created you to enjoy. He doesn't want you to feel ashamed or uncomfortable with the body he gave you.

Almost every book I read in my research discussed the importance of "self-discovery." You and I need to understand how our bodies work. We need to feel comfortable touching ourselves to discover how God made us. Is this masturbation? Dr. Rosenau identifies this as genital pleasuring. In the context of a loving, sexual relationship, it's simply a part of your sexual experience as a couple.

Is masturbation or self-pleasuring wrong when it's in the context of your sexual relationship? The Bible is silent on this subject. Dr. Douglas Rosenau addresses this by looking at several scriptures (Genesis 38, Romans

14:14, and 1 Corinthians 6:12). He concludes that self-pleasuring is permissible with these cautions: (1) It cannot become a habitual act that detracts from making love and locks in a type of arousal your mate cannot duplicate. (2) Guarding your fantasy and thought life is essential, because this is where we can cross over God's guidelines about lust. (3) It cannot undermine the intimate companionship of marital oneness.[39]

Clifford and Joyce Penner address this in *The Gift of Sex* by suggesting that you filter it through the question, "Is this a loving act?" They conclude, "If one partner desires a great deal of sexual activity and the other is less frequently interested, the couple might decide that masturbation is the most loving act the highly interested person can do."[40]

What About Anal Sex?

The Bible is silent on this, but there are some very important health issues that need to be considered. Dr. Rosenau cautions, "The vaginal tissue was designed by God for intercourse and the anus was not. It is easy to sustain tears and lesions in the rectal tissue. Also many bacteria in the anus can interfere with the bacterial balance in the vagina and cause infections." While it is a matter to be decided completely between a husband and a wife, these considerations need to be taken into account.[41]

What's Not Okay in Bed?

God gives incredible sexual freedom within the boundaries of the marital relationship. At the same time, he also prohibits certain sexual behaviors. In the same way that a parent establishes rules and boundaries to protect a child, God's sexual boundaries are in place to protect us from harm.

In preparing for their book *Intimate Issues,* Linda Dillow and Lorraine Pintus read the Bible from front to back, compiling a list of every scriptural reference to sex. In their research here are the ten things God forbids:

1. *Fornication:* Fornication is immoral sex, which includes sex outside of marriage, incest, prostitution, and adultery (Matthew 5:32; 1 Corinthians 5:1; 6:13, 15–16; 7:2; 1 Thessalonians 4:3).
2. *Adultery:* Adultery is when a married person has sex with someone other than their spouse (Leviticus 20:10; Matthew 5:28).
3. *Homosexuality:* The Bible is very clear that a man having sex with a man or a woman having sex with a woman is detestable to God (Leviticus 18:22, 20:13; Romans 1:27; 1 Corinthians 6:9).
4. *Impurity:* To become "impure" can mean to lose one's virginity or to choose to live an ungodly or unholy lifestyle (1 Corinthians 6:9; 2 Corinthians 7:1; Revelation 14:4, 22:11).
5. *Orgies:* For a married couple to become involved in sex orgies with other couples is fornication, adultery, and impurity as discussed above (Romans 13:13; Galatians 5:21; 1 Peter 4:3).
6. *Prostitution:* Prostitution is paying for sex (Leviticus 19:29; Deuteronomy 23:17; Proverbs 7:4–27).
7. *Lustful passions:* Lust is the unrestrained, indiscriminate sexual desire for men or women other than the person's spouse (Mark 7:21–22; Ephesians 4:19).
8. *Sodomy:* The biblical word sodomy refers to men lying with men. In the Bible, sodomites refer to male homosexuals or male temple prostitutes.
9. *Obscenity and coarse jokes:* Although this does not rule out appropriate sexual humor in the privacy of marriage, it does apply to inappropriate sexual comments in a public setting (Ephesians 4:29, 5:4).
10. *Incest:* Incest is sex with family members or relatives (Leviticus 18:7–18; 20:11–21).[42]

Do you see how the above would rob you of the sexual pleasure God created for your marriage? His boundaries are for our protection, both emotionally and physically.

A Celebration of Sex

God provided married couples with a pleasurable, intimate, perfect gift to unwrap together—sexual intercourse. Some of us have gazed at the gift, admired its beautiful wrapping paper, but have barely removed the ribbon and bow. Others have unwrapped the gift and enjoyed it fully.

What have you done with God's gift of sex? Is the wrapping paper still on your gift? Have you partially unwrapped the gift, but not yet discovered what's really inside? Have you opened your present and been enjoying the gift for quite some time? God's gift of sex in marriage is unique because it keeps on giving. Just when you think you've unwrapped it and enjoyed the gift completely, you discover another facet to enjoy! Unwrap, enjoy, and celebrate!

Personal Reflections

1. THINK of two ways you can improve bringing pleasure to your husband. Determine how and when you will experiment with these new ideas.

2. IDENTIFY any misconceptions you had about God's design for sex. Thank him for his beautiful gift and ask him to help you open more layers of it every day of your marriage.

3. Do you struggle more with giving pleasure or receiving pleasure? Ask God to help you move forward in the area you struggle with most.

For Husbands Only

This chapter focused on the fine art of pleasuring. As men, you and I often focus on the goal of intercourse and eventually the release of orgasm. However, if we want to truly enjoy the sexual pleasures God has given us in our marriage, we have to change our goal from intercourse to pleasure.

To fully experience God's plan for sexual intimacy, we have to understand the importance of giving and receiving pleasure. We have to become a sexual connoisseur, always looking for ways to improve our wives' lovemaking experiences.

This chapter is full of sexual technique suggestions. Check out some of the subtitles and read the sections that interest you the most. Make sure you understand the importance of your wife's most important sex organ: the clitoris (see page 164). Ask your wife what she learned from the chapter and be ready to learn things about her you might not have known. You and I need to be students of our wives, always looking to deepen our emotional and physical intimacy.

Here's to the fine art of pleasuring. May we have many opportunities to perfect it!

Mark

Desire Details

WHILE WRITING THIS BOOK, Mark and I spent some time together, taking our own advice to get away on a regular basis without the kids. In doing so, we weathered the comments of friends and family who knew of this writing project and humorously wanted to know if we were taking some time "for research" or "to conduct a field study" for my book.

Our reason for getting away was multifaceted, but writing this book has been a research experiment in and of itself. Although I never gave much thought to how immersing myself in this subject might affect my marriage, I'll be the first to admit that the results have been surprising.

We experienced an intense increase in my sexual desire while writing the book. They say men think about sex once every seventeen seconds; this contributes to their higher drive. According to my friend Jane, women think about sex once every seventeen days—and that's on a good month! Most women don't have the same drive or desire as their husbands because we do not think about it as much. I have not only increased my reading about the topic, but I have also moved from thinking about sex once every seventeen days to thinking about it during much of the day. I have discovered a direct correlation between thoughts and desire. Mark wants to know if I can write about this subject for the rest of our married life!

In reality, most couples are always dealing with a difference of opinion when it comes to the frequency of their intimate relations. If you expect to reach a point in marriage where you both will be sharing the same level of desire, you are probably going to be waiting a long time!

There are still questions that remain: What if I have less desire than my husband? Or more? Most couples find they have to compromise on sexual frequency. What do I do if I don't feel sexy? How can creativity increase desire? What can we do to keep from getting in a lovemaking rut? Before we bring this discussion to a close, we need to explore the "desire details."

I'm Less Interested in Sex than My Spouse

What strategies help if you have less desire than your husband? Try some of these ideas in handling your differences.

Keep Balance in Your Life

As women, you and I are capable of spinning many plates at once. However, if we need to give extra energy to our marriages (and particularly the physical relationship), we may be spread too thin to give them the attention they need.

Create an Environment that Helps You Transition from Mom to Wife

If you know that a warm bath in a candlelit room relaxes you and helps you focus on your sexual needs, make the effort to make it happen.

Pay Attention to Subtle Sexual Cues
in Your Own Body

You may have turned off the "sex" button a long time ago, but God created you to enjoy sexual pleasure. Pay attention to what prompts any thoughts of romance or making love. Strategize ways to maximize those thoughts regardless of how subtle they might be!

Focus on Bringing Pleasure to Your Spouse

Your focus on bringing pleasure to your spouse will supercede your lack of desire. Sometimes when you focus on pleasing him, your desire follows.

Don't Feel Guilty When You Need to Say No

When you need to say no, do so assuring your spouse you will respond to his request for intimacy. You don't have to feel guilty when saying no, as long as you communicate to your spouse your sincere desire to fulfill his request. A simple no is not an honoring response. If you can respond with, "I'm very tired tonight and do not feel I can give you my all. I'd like to commit to intimacy tomorrow night when I will have had a bit more sleep. Would that be okay with you?" Then keep your word and prepare yourself to give and receive love.

Exercise Your PC Muscle Using Kegel Exercises

If you gave birth vaginally you were probably encouraged to use Kegel exercises to strengthen your pubococcygeal (PC) muscle, which surrounds the opening of the vagina and anus. Did you know that exercising this muscle can also increase sexual desire? To locate this muscle, practice stopping the flow of urine. Once you understand how to flex the muscle, you can exercise it when you're in the car, talking on the phone, or watching TV. Need to increase desire? Exercise that PC muscle of yours![43]

I'm More Interested in Sex than My Husband Is

We've talked extensively about the gender differences in sex and even generalized that men are more interested than women. Research supports that premise. However, there certainly are exceptions to the rule. You may be one of them.

Teri found herself feeling very unattractive in her sixth month of pregnancy. She wanted more than anything else to feel that her husband, Bob, still found her attractive. Although Bob routinely desired sex less often than Teri, her heightened emotional state misread his lack of interest. She measured her appearance based upon her husband's interest, which was coming up very short.

Carole and John found themselves in a similar situation. John simply did not have a strong physical drive for sex. While he enjoyed their sexual relationship, it was Carole who more often initiated their lovemaking. John was affectionate and loving, just less interested sexually than his wife.

Both of these situations represent normal marriage situations. If you are the initiator more often than your husband, you are not alone. While the percentages may be smaller, many couples do find that she is more interested than he.

What do you do if this is your situation? Start with the following suggestions.

Learn What Excites Your Husband

What is it that gets his sexual motor running? What is the "on" button? Find out what activities help him anticipate and desire making love.

Respect His Preconditions for Lovemaking

You may have a creative streak, while he is more traditional or even inhibited. If so, love him where he is, respecting his desires. Your unconditional acceptance will build trust that eventually can be turned into a safe, secure relationship that allows for expanding the sexual boundaries.

Don't Take Rejection Personally

When your partner needs to say no, it's probably not about you at all. It's about a lack of energy, a distracted mind, or some other factor that would keep him from giving his all to you.

Communicate Openly

In addition to these suggestions, an increase in communication can help. Teri shared with Bob her insecurities concerning her growing belly and changing appearance. She told him that she felt unattractive and that she was reading his lack of interest in sex as a confirmation of her feelings. Bob didn't realize how insecure Teri was about her appearance during pregnancy. Her communication allowed him to better communicate that he found her attractive; it also prompted him to initiate sex more often, now knowing how important it was for her emotionally.

I Don't Feel Very Sexy

I have never felt very sexy. Period. Even before I had children, I don't know that I ever felt really comfortable with my body or seductive in my marriage. Yet I have learned that much of that is my own narrow mind-set, largely affected by my misconceptions and incorrect attitudes about my sexuality.

I hope that by now you have a sense of your sexual identity according to God. My prayer is that you realize his unique design for you as a female created to enjoy sexual pleasure. Now we have to recognize the battle that plays in our minds that keeps us from feeling sexy.

After four pregnancies my belly looks like a zebra's striped coat. My cesarean scar is tucked under the stripes as if it were underlining a word to make a point. The cellulite on my legs jiggles when I walk. And my husband finds me attractive? Yes, he does. I'm the one who has the insecurity problem about feeling sensual.

Once we understand God's perspective about his wonderful gift of sex, what can we do to increase our desire and move past our inhibitions? How can we make love with vigor and confidence? What strategies can we put in place to take our lovemaking to the next level? The ideas are endless, but we'll explore just a few to get you started.

Update Your Bedroom Attire

So you sleep in your husband's old t-shirt? We'll start there. How about something pretty and feminine? Something a little revealing? Okay, how about something that is completely sensual?

For years I was uncomfortable wearing sexy lingerie. I always blamed it on the clothes (or lack thereof). Now I know that I wasn't really uncomfortable with the clothes; I was uncomfortable with my own sexuality.

How about investing in a private sexual wardrobe? Personally, I hate anything with lace. I have sensitive skin and find most lace to be irritating to my skin. But not every sexy nightgown is made with lace. Look for what works for you but stretches your comfort zone as well.

Use your imagination and think beyond basic lingerie. How about a robe with a matching bra and panty underneath? A tuxedo shirt with nothing else? A tank top with a matching thong? The possibilities are endless! Check out www.integrityintimates.com to shop for intimate apparel and romantic products from a Christian company.

Now consider how you might take it off in a seductive, inviting manner. Maybe you invite him to undress you. Remember, God created this for satisfaction, enjoyment, and pleasure. It's a form of recreation for a husband and wife. Have fun playing together!

Change Your Underwear

Okay, I hope you change your underwear every day. That's not what I'm talking about here. Have you fallen into the habit of wearing a basic white, boring bra? Be honest. Have you succumbed to the panty that covers your belly button? I know they're great for comfort, but they won't do much for helping you feel sexy.

Invest in some colored undergarments. If you've never had a matching bra and panty set, pick up a couple. Ever tried a thong? You might like it!

It's amazing how pretty underwear can help you begin to feel sexy. One mom shared that her husband loves to see her in a black capri outfit she purchased. She decided to invest in a black bra and panty set that she always wears under it. It's their little secret. He goes crazy just thinking about the black underwear she's wearing, and her sexy undergarments keep her thinking about the sexual intimacy they will most likely share at the end of the day. It's a win-win situation for both of them.

Are You in the Mood?

Many couples find their methods of communicating sexual desire less than ideal. Have you established some "code language" or nonverbal indicators that help you communicate when you're in the mood for love?

My friend Karen shared that she and her husband, Todd, keep two candles in their bedroom, one on each side of their bed. When he's in the mood, he lights his candle. When she's in the mood, she lights her candle. Karen humorously added, "When I'm really *not* in the mood, I hide all the matches!"

If you have never determined a good way to communicate sexual interest, consider adding some creativity to your communication. Brainstorm some ideas and decide together if you want to do something different in the communication department. I'm not at all advocating hinting here. Hinting *anything* in marriage is a poor form of communication. I'm talking about your unique way to communicate sexual desire. You may both just enjoy a straight verbal request—if so, that's fine. However, if you've never discussed creatively communicating the need, you might be missing some fun!

When it comes to being in the mood, if you don't initiate sex very often—surprise your husband with a request for intimacy on occasion. This will take the predictability out of your relationship. Watching him respond to your invitation will be worth all the courage you muster up to initiate the lovemaking.

Change Your Perspective

What is the most important sexual organ? It's the brain. Knowing this, one of the places we can increase our desire is by changing our perspective. Consider sex your opportunity to do something other than the daily responsibilities of motherhood. Think of it as an adventure or an opportunity for fun.

In the book *Fit to Be Tied*, Lynne Hybels talks about how her sexual relationship with her husband, Bill, turned around when she changed her perspective:

> Diapers, Dinner, Dishes, Sex. They were all part of the same routine, all part of my responsibility as a wife and mother. And all about equally enjoyable.
>
> But somewhere along the way I began to see sex differently. I began to view it as a diversion, an escape, a chance to crawl out from under routine responsibilities and mundane chores. A chance to put on a new hat, to be somebody different. A chance to have some fun right in my own home, without having to buy a ticket or pay a babysitter. I began to view it as a break that I deserved, a romantic reward.
>
> When I began to view sex as something fun I could do for myself . . . I became a much more exciting sexual partner.[44]

I would have to agree with Lynne. I truly believe one of the biggest changes that has happened in my approach to sex is changing my perspective from something I am doing for Mark to something I am doing for me as well. You and I need to keep our perspective balanced. As Bill and Lynne put it, "We're not talking about selfish sex.... What we're talking about is authentic, fully engaged, mutually enjoyable, genuinely fun sex."[45]

Create a Sensual Environment

The environment we create can be a definite desire booster. If you haven't given much thought to the environment of your bedroom, do a little evaluation. Does it encourage variety? Is it comfortable and inviting? Do you have the ability to play music? Incorporate different lighting? Can you creatively use mirrors to increase visual excitement? Have any lotions and oils on hand? These are just a few ideas to help you create a sensual environment.

If you don't have a CD player in your bedroom, consider making the investment. I've seen "boom box" CD players for as low as $25, and you can now purchase radio/alarm/CD players, which are perfect for the bedroom! Purchase a couple of instrumental CDs for your lovemaking experience. Piano or saxophone music are great options. Different styles of music, such as ballads, jazz, or orchestra, can also add to romantic creativity. You might even want to enjoy a bit of slow-dancing to get you started!

What about the lighting in your room? Do you have a dimmer switch on your light? How about candlelight? Do you keep a few candles in your bedroom? Flickering candlelight gives ambiance. Even leaving the light on in an adjoining bathroom with the door ajar can give just enough light to tantalize the eyes.

Many spouses enjoy caressing each other with lotions or oils. These enhance the sensation of touch as well as the sense of smell if they have a pleasing aroma. Perfume or cologne can add to the ambiance as well. Consider your bed linens. Is it time to invest in some new bedding to create a warm, inviting, special environment for lovemaking?

Schedule It!

The concept of spontaneous sex is wonderful in a world without children. You may have experienced that before children and someday you'll be able to enjoy it again after the children leave your home, but during the season of childrearing you can't depend on spontaneity.

When Mark and I determined to make changes in our marriage, one of the first things we did was schedule our sex life. You're probably thinking that it sounds so clinical, so cold. I did. In reality, however, we found a new layer of intimacy in our marriage. We discovered that when we planned our times together, we anticipated them. There was a new sense of excitement and adventure in our relationship.

How did we make this happen? With an infant in the house, we would work around naptime—maximizing the first hour of deep sleep on a Saturday afternoon. As the kids entered preschool, we found a long lunch hour every Tuesday to work very well. In one season of parenting we traded sitting with some friends and made Friday night our time. Now that all the kids are in school and Mark has Fridays off, Friday is our special day. Don't call us or drop by our house that day because we won't answer the phone, and we certainly won't answer the door! We're focused on each other. We've set boundaries in place to protect our marriage, and we've planned for times of fun.

Does this mean lovemaking doesn't happen at other times of the week? Absolutely not. There are certainly spontaneous occasions to give and receive love. Scheduling it, however, assures us of time to have fun, experiment, and prioritize our lovemaking.

Consider Yourself a Life-Long Learner

Becoming great lovers is an acquired skill. While some people are more natural lovers, we all need to think of ourselves as learners. Invest in a good Christian book on sexual technique. Read about marriage and allow the new information to transform your heart and your mind. Be willing to change. When making love, try something new and ask your husband if he liked it. Take risks. Learn. Try.

Be a student of your spouse. Study his likes and dislikes. Pay attention to what excites him when you are making love. Explore new touches, new environments, and different love-making positions. Think of yourself as a life-long learner and approach each love-making opportunity as a time to apply your new knowledge.

Be Creative!

Looking to increase desire? Let the creative ideas flow! You are restricted only by your lack of creativity.

I believe every married couple should own *Simply Romantic Nights*, a creative resource developed by Family Life (www.familylife.com). The box of twenty-four sealed envelopes is designed to rekindle the flames of passion in your relationship. Each envelope suggests a romantic adventure (twelve for him and twelve for her) to keep the excitement burning in your marriage. Sometimes we need a little help incorporating variety into our romance and lovemaking. Christian resources such as this help with the creativity, while respecting God's design for sexual intimacy.

Be creative about putting the sizzle into your marriage. Build anticipation, pleasure each other, share fantasies, romance each other, and experience God's beautiful gift of sex.

The Final Answer to the Question

What a journey we've been on! We've explored this intricate relationship called marriage. We've looked at

God's plan for sexual intimacy. We've discussed the importance of having a marriage-centered family. We've talked about differences and finding them fascinating rather than frustrating. We've evaluated our thought patterns and their effect on our marriages. We've discovered God's gift of giving and receiving pleasure. We've developed strategies for increasing desire and bringing new life to our sexual relationship.

Is there really sex after kids? You bet! It's more exciting and more incredible than most of us have experienced! I hope you enjoy spending the rest of your life opening new layers of this wonderful gift of intimacy in marriage.

I leave you with these words from God's heart:

> I belong to my lover, and his desire is for me.
> Come, my lover, let us go to the countryside,
> Let us spend the night in the villages.
> Let us go early to the vineyards to see if the vines
>   have budded, if their blossoms have opened,
>   and if the pomegranates are in bloom—
> There I will give you my love.
> (Song of Solomon 7:10–12)

Personal Reflections

1. Now that you are on the last chapter of this book, have you found that while reading this book, your desire has increased at all? Identify two ways you can increase the amount of time and energy you give to your sexual relationship.

2. If you have less desire than your husband, choose two of the ideas on pages 178–79 to implement increasing your desire. If you have more desire than your husband, which suggestion on pages 180–81 most applies to you?

3. Where can you make a change in the next week: your bedroom attire, your underclothes, or your bedroom environment? What change will you make and when will you make it?

4. Write out the scripture at the end of this chapter on an index card and place it somewhere where you will see it everyday.

For Husbands Only

Jill and I have always had differing levels of sexual desire, and how we've handled those differences has not always been honoring to each other. This chapter focused on how to handle our different desire levels. You'll want to check out pages 178–81 to find the section that most likely applies to you.

I used to rarely give any thought to bedroom attire for myself (am I wearing an old torn t-shirt or something with a bit more class?) or to the bedroom environment (music, candles, etc). Now I understand how important these things are. Even my own personal hygiene can make a difference in my wife's response to me physically (have I brushed my teeth, taken a shower, or shaven?).

This book has been a journey to deeper marital intimacy. We've looked at God's plan for sexual intimacy. We've talked about differences and finding them fascinating rather than frustrating. We've discussed the importance of being marriage-centered rather than child-centered. We've discovered God's gift of giving and receiving pleasure. We've learned that helping around the house and with the kids is where sex really begins hours and days before we make love.

I encourage you to take your wife away to enjoy some time just for the two of you. Consider attending a marriage retreat together to continue exploring the depths of your relationship. Step up and take the lead in making your marriage the priority.

Is there sex after kids? There sure is, and it's more exciting and more incredible than most of us have experienced. Here's to enjoying the rest of your life opening new layers of the unique gift of intimacy in marriage!

Mark

Marriage Resources

Websites

www.aacc.net—The American Association of Christian Counselors website can connect you to an accredited counselor in your area.

www.divorcecare.org—This organization helps people find healing from the hurts of divorce.

www.healinghearts.org—The Healing Hearts Ministry is committed to helping couples find healing from abortion.

www.hearts-at-home.org—Hearts at Home is an organization committed to encouraging, educating, and equipping mothers at home in their family relationships.

www.integrityintimates.com—This website is a moral, non-pornographic online lingerie boutique where both husband and wife can safely enjoy purchasing intimate apparel and romantic products.

www.marriagealive.com—Committed to helping people build strong marriage and family relationships.

www.marriagepartnership.com—Marriage Partnership offers encouraging articles and resources for Christian marriages.

www.smalley.gospelcom.net—The Smalley Relationship Center offers deep care for the marriage relationship through conferences, products, and counseling.

Magazines

Marriage Partnership—Published by Christianity Today, this quarterly magazine offers realistic help for making marriage everything God intends, based on shared faith, sexual fidelity, lifelong commitment, sacrificial love, and mutual respect. Contact Hearts at Home for special subscription rates.

Marriage Seminars and Retreats

ABC's of a Healthy Marriage Seminar—This seminar is offered twice a year in central Illinois. Friday evenings and all-day Saturday seminars offer practical advice to growing a healthy marriage. Call 309-829-2275 for more info.

"I Still Do" Marriage Seminar—Also sponsored by Family Life, "I Still Do" events are one-day arena events designed to help couples refocus on their marital relationship. Call 1-800-FLToday to find the next event in your area.

Marriage for a Lifetime and Real Love in the Real World—These marriage seminars, offered by the Smalley Relationship Center, help couples inject encouragement, excitement and energy into their marriages. Call 1-800-848-6329 or visit their website at www.smalley.gospelcom.net.

A Weekend to Remember Marriage Conference—Sponsored by Family Life, this three-day getaway for husbands and wives offers practical advice for making marriage all God intended it to be. Call 1-800-FLToday for a conference in your area.

United Marriage Encounter—These weekend retreats help put the spark back in your marriage relationship. Call 1-800-334-8920 for more information.

Bibles

Couples Devotional Bible
Life Application Bible
NIV Study Bible

Books

Sexual Relationship

David and Claudia Arp, *Love Life for Parents*
Kay Arthur, *Sex ... According to God*
Robert and Rosemary Barnes, *Great Sexpectations*
Linda Dillow and Lorraine Pintus, *Intimate Issues*

Tim Gardner, *Sacred Sex*

Family Life Ministry, *Simply Romantic Nights*

Tim and Beverly LaHaye, *The Act of Marriage* and *The Act of Marriage After 40*

Tommy Nelson, *The Book of Romance*

Clifford and Joyce Penner, *The Gift of Sex* and *Restoring the Pleasure*

Douglas Rosenau, *A Celebration of Sex*

Ed Wheat, *Intended for Pleasure* and *Love Life for Every Married Couple*

Marriage

Gary Chapman, *The Five Love Languages*

Willard Harley, *His Needs, Her Needs*

Bill and Lynne Hybels, *Fit to Be Tied*

Les and Leslie Parrott, *Questions Couples Ask*

Bobbie and Myron Yagel, *15 Minutes to Build a Stronger Marriage*

Motherhood

Allie Pleiter, *Becoming a Chief Home Officer*

Jill Savage, *Professionalizing Motherhood*

In-Depth Counseling and Marriage Help

Blessing Ranch—This Christian leader resource and renewal center specializes in helping Christian leaders and couples find healing from the hurts of their past. Visit www.blessingranch.org for more information.

Couples Intensive Program—This intensive, highly focused, time-limited counseling approach allows couples to get away from the normal daily distractions that often keep them from having the time and energy to find each other, let alone solutions to their problems. The therapists work with couples in one, two or four day blocks to help them identify their struggles and find strategies to make healing changes. Call 1-866-875-2915 for more information or visit their website at www.smalley.gospelcom.net.

Who I Am According to God

Accepted

John 1:12—I am God's child.

John 15:15—I am Christ's friend.

Romans 5:1—I have been justified.

1 Corinthians 6:17—I am united with the Lord, and I am one spirit with him.

1 Corinthians 6:19–20—I have been bought with a price. I belong to God.

1 Corinthians 12:27—I am a member of Christ's body.

Ephesians 1:1—I am a saint.

Ephesians 1:5—I have been adopted as God's child.

Ephesians 2:18—I have direct access to God through the Holy Spirit.

Colossians 1:14—I have been redeemed and forgiven of all my sins.

Colossians 2:10—I am complete in Christ.

Secure

Romans 8:1–2—I am forever free from condemnation.

Romans 8:28—I am assured that all things work together for good.

Romans 8:31–34—I am free from any condemning charges against me.

Romans 8:35–39—I cannot be separated from the love of God.

2 Corinthians 1:21–22—I have been established, anointed, and sealed by God.

Colossians 3:3—I am hidden with Christ in God.

Philippians 1:6—I am confident that the good work that God has begun in me will be perfected.

Philippians 3:20—I am a citizen of heaven.

2 Timothy 1:7—I have not been given a spirit of fear but of power, love, and a sound mind.

Hebrews 4:16—I can find grace and mercy in time of need.

1 John 5:18—I am born of God, and the evil one cannot touch me.

Significant

Matthew 5:13–14—I am the salt of the earth and the light of the world.

John 15:1, 5—I am a branch of the true vine, a channel of his life.

John 15:16—I have been chosen and appointed to bear fruit.

Acts 1:8—I am a personal witness of Christ's.

1 Corinthians 3:16—I am God's temple.

2 Corinthians 5:17–21—I am a minister of reconciliation for God.

2 Corinthians 6:1—I am God's coworker (1 Corinthians 3:9).

Ephesians 2:6—I am seated with Christ in the heavenly realm.

Ephesians 2:10—I am God's workmanship.

Ephesians 3:12—I may approach God with freedom and confidence.

Philippians 4:13—I can do all things through Christ who strengthens me.

---

*This appendix has been taken from Neil Anderson's *Victory Over the Darkness* (Regal).

Notes

1. NIV Study Bible Introduction: Song of Songs (Grand Rapids: Zondervan, 1985), 1004.

2. Douglas Rosenau, *A Celebration of Sex* (Nashville: Nelson, 1994), 21.

3. Ibid., 106.

4. Brian Jamison and Heather Jamison, "Haunted by Premarital Sex," *Marriage Partnership* (Spring 2001), 22–26.

5. Clifford Penner and Joyce Penner, *The Gift of Sex* (Dallas: Word, 1981), 12.

6. Rosenau, *A Celebration of Sex*, 17.

7. Linda Dillow and Lorraine Pintus, *Intimate Issues* (Colorado Springs: Waterbrook, 1999), 166.

8. Adapted from Dillow and Pintus, *Intimate Issues*, 167–68.

9. Rosenau, *In Celebration of Sex*, 333.

10. Archibald Hart, *The Sexual Man* (Waco, Tex.: Word, 1994), 95.

11. Leslie Vernick, *How To Act Right When Your Spouse Acts Wrong* (Colorado Springs: Waterbrook, 2001), 6.

12. Ibid.

13. Mike Mason, *The Mystery of Marriage* (Sisters, Oreg.: Multnomah, 1985), 119.

14. Rosenau, *A Celebration of Sex*, 27.

15. Myron Yagel and Bobbie Yagel, *Fifteen Minutes to a Stronger Marriage* (Wheaton, Ill.: Tyndale, 1995), 60.

16. Adapted from Yagel and Yagel, *Fifteen Minutes to a Stronger Marriage*, 60–61.

17. David Arp and Claudia Arp, *Love Life for Parents* (Grand Rapids: Zondervan, 1998), 124.

18. Robert Barnes and Rosemary Barnes, *Great Sexpectations* (Grand Rapids: Zondervan, 1996), 201–2.

19. Dave Meurer, *Daze of Our Wives* (Minneapolis: Bethany, 2000).

20. Vernick, *How To Act Right When Your Spouse Acts Wrong*, 66.

21. Ibid.

22. Ibid., 40.

23. Rob Marus, "Kiss Nonsense Goodbye," *Christianity Today* (June 11, 2001), 48.

24. Mike Mason, *The Mystery of Marriage*, 129.

25. Willard Harley, *His Needs, Her Needs* (Grand Rapids: Revell, 1986).

26. Gary Smalley, *Making Love Last Forever* (Nashville: W Publishing, 1996), 236.

27. Rosenau, *A Celebration of Sex*, 190.

28. Ibid., 190.

29. Ibid., 21.

30. Adapted from Rosenau, *A Celebration of Sex*, 37–38.

31. Ibid., 42.

32. Penner and Penner, *The Gift of Sex*, 60.

33. Rosenau, *A Celebration of Sex*, 107.

34. Ibid., 52.

35. Ibid.

36. Joyce Penner, "What Every Woman Needs to Know About Sexual Satisfaction," *Marriage Partnership* (Winter 2001), 38.

37. Adapted from Penner, "What Every Woman Needs to Know About Sexual Satisfaction," 38–39.

38. Penner and Penner, *The Gift of Sex*, 182.

39. Rosenau, *A Celebration of Sex*, 152–53.

40. Penner and Penner, *The Gift of Sex*, 234.

41. Rosenau, *A Celebration of Sex*, 181.

42. Adapted from Dillow and Pintus, *Intimate Issues*, 199–200.

43. Rosenau, *A Celebration of Sex*, 194.

44. Bill Hybels and Lynne Hybels, *Fit to Be Tied* (Grand Rapids: Zondervan, 1991), 170–71.

45. Ibid., 171.

Leader's Guide

Introduction

A discussion group for moms provides a wonderful opportunity for personal growth, friendship, and encouragement. Women in the profession of motherhood can struggle with isolation if they do not have regular networking opportunities. They can feel unappreciated without a pat on the back every once in a while. And they can lose vision if they are not reminded of the importance of the job they are doing. This leader's guide is designed to stimulate the building of relationships that will encourage, equip, and educate moms. Whether your group is a small group that meets in your living room, or a larger moms' group, or a MOPS group that meets in a church or community building, the most important aspect of gathering together is intentionally building relationships.

Preparing to Lead

First, pray for the women in your group and for God's guidance as you lead the group.

Take some time each week before the group meets to familiarize yourself with the discussion agenda. Make notes on additional questions you might present to the group. Create a list of items you need to remember to bring to the meeting. Consider creating a "study basket" specifically for keeping items you will need each week. Pens, highlighters, name tags, index cards, notebook paper, and your copy of the book would be basic essentials. When special items are needed for a specific week, just drop them in the basket and you'll be sure to remember them!

You'll notice that every discussion has four parts each playing an important role in meaningful interaction with the content and in relationship building. Let's take a quick look at the purpose of each part.

Icebreaker

When your group first gets together each week, you will find it beneficial to start out with a light-hearted,

get-to-know-you-better activity. Each mom has probably had a hectic time just getting to the group, and she
may be preoccupied with thoughts of child care, household chores that are going undone, or juggling this
week's carpool responsibilities or extra-curricular activities. The 10–15 minute Icebreaker is designed to focus
everyone on the people around them and the topic at
hand. It fosters relationships and builds a sense of
camaraderie through laughing and sharing together.

When you finish up the Icebreaker time, open the discussion part of your meeting with prayer. Commit your
time to the Lord and ask him to lead your discussion.

Dig Deep

The best moms' groups are not led by leaders who like
to hear themselves talk, but rather by leaders who draw
out the thoughts of others. The questions in Dig Deep are
designed to facilitate discussion rather than teach a lesson
and will probably take about 30–45 minutes.

Don't feel confined by the questions listed in the leader's
guide. If you believe another line of questions better fits
your group, adjust the discussion to fit your group's needs.
You might also refer to the personal reflection questions
at the end of each chapter for further ideas.

Because this subject is sensitive in nature, it is important to keep some boundaries in your group discussions.
You should never share with others intimate details
about your sexual relationship with your husband. In
other words, no one should ever be able to imagine you
and your husband in bed. A reassuring conversation with
your husband might be helpful as you commit to keep
your physical relationship private. Keep the group discussions as focused on God as possible. Share what God
is teaching you about himself and about his perspective
on the sexual relationship. Discuss how you are changing
as you learn more about God's beautiful gift of sexual
intimacy.

During the group's discussion time your job will be to draw out the women. You will most likely have some women who want to monopolize the discussion and some who hardly say a word on their own. To draw out the woman who is quieter, you may find it useful to ask her some questions specifically to help her join the discussion. When a group member has the habit of monopolizing conversations, keep the discussion moving by calling on other women immediately after you pose a question. If the group gets off the subject in their discussions, simply pull the focus back to the original question posed.

Apply

The true benefit of reading this book and discussing it with others is not to simply absorb new information, but rather to experience positive changes in daily life. The Apply section is designed to stimulate personal application and provide the opportunity for the moms to share how they have been challenged or moved to action. Some participants may want to invite one another to hold them accountable to make the changes God is impressing upon them, or commit to encouraging one another through challenging change. Others may discover life-changing implications they would have never thought of on their own. This vitally important part of the discussion may take approximately 10–20 minutes to complete.

Pray

Prayer may be either invigorating or intimidating, depending on a person's understanding and experience with prayer. If the moms in your group are comfortable praying together, take some time at the end of your group to pray together about the things you have learned. As the leader, take the responsibility of closing out the prayer time when the group seems to be finished praying or when the clock requires that you end your time together.

If your group is not comfortable praying together, then close the group in prayer yourself or ask another member of the group who is comfortable praying aloud to do so. The prayer suggestions are simply suggestions. Pray whatever God lays on your heart to pray. There is no right or wrong when it comes to prayer; simply talk to God as you would talk to a friend.

Assignments and Notes

In some chapters you may find an assignment for the next week or notes to help your planning. These will help you gather together any items that might be needed in the next chapter or the coming weeks.

It is a core value of Hearts at Home to provide resources to moms, moms' groups, and moms' group leaders. We hope this book provides you the opportunity to interact with women who are doing the same job you are doing. Our goal is that this, and other Hearts at Home resources will encourage, educate, and equip women in the profession of motherhood!

Chapter One: God Created Sex!

Icebreaker
Ask each person to share with the group how she met her husband and where they went on their first date.

Dig Deep
1. In what ways have you misunderstood God's plan for the sexual relationship in marriage? Like the author, have you understood only one piece of the plan? With which part of God's plan are you most comfortable? Which part is a stretch?

2. Have you ever considered the sexual relationship as an opportunity for a husband and wife to play together? Does that thought excite you or intimidate you?

3. Read Song of Solomon 5:10–16. Now read 5:9 and answer the question asked in verse 9. What is one physical trait first attracted you to your husband? Name one character trait that drew you to him.

4. Did anyone read Song of Solomon together with her husband this week? Invite anyone who did so to share her experience of reading the Bible together. Was it uncomfortable? Was it encouraging? Did it help initiate conversation?

Apply

1. Identify two ways you can make a shift in your thinking about God's gift of sex.

2. Find one Bible verse in this chapter that you can—or will—write on an index card and keep as a reminder of God's truth about sex.

3. Read Song of Solomon this week if you haven't already done so.

Pray
Thank God for the husband he has given to each mom in the group.

Thank God for the gift of sex and ask him to show you more about his plan for the sexual relationship in marriage.

Ask God to be your official travel guide on this journey of marriage. Commit to trust his lead and follow his ways.

Chapter Two: Intimacy Inhibitors

Icebreaker
Ask participants to tell the group where they went on their honeymoons. Ask them to share one special memory they have of their time away. Be sensitive to anyone in the group who did not have a traditional trip.

Dig Deep
1. Take the lead in telling the group of one suitcase you carried into your marital relationship. Ask the group: With what suitcase do you most identify and why?

2. What is the difference between a half apology and a full apology? Identify what keeps us from resolving conflict fully.

3. Read Joel 2:25. Discuss how this scripture applies to the marital relationship.

Apply

1. Identify one action point you will take from this chapter. What will your first step be in unpacking a suitcase or finding healing? Share this with the group.

2. As the group leader, if you are comfortable doing so, express your willingness to be a safe place of love and encouragement for any woman in the group who needs to talk about a major challenge she is facing in her marriage. Offer to meet one-on-one if she is uncomfortable sharing within the group.

3. Discuss the marriage and counseling resources available in your community or in a nearby city. Check out the American Association of Christian Counselors website to find a Christian counselor near you (www.aacc.net).

Pray

Pray specifically for any mom who has revealed difficulties about her marriage or her past. Ask God to give her direction in finding the healing needed.

Thank God for his grace and forgiveness to cover our past mistakes and the mistakes of others.

Ask God to help you focus less on your husband's shortcomings and more on the areas in which God wants you to grow.

Leader Assignment

Bring index cards to the next meeting.

Chapter Three: And Then I Had Kids

Icebreaker

Have each mom tell the group about her birthing or adoption experience. Any humorous stories? Surprises?

Dig Deep

1. Of the five sexual intimacy challenges mentioned in this chapter (fatigue, pregnancy, nursing, birth control, and the presence of children), which do you most identify with today? When it comes to sexual intimacy, have you found any challenges associated with motherhood not mentioned by the author?

2. Ask each woman in the group to share one strategy she finds helpful in mentally preparing for lovemaking.

3. Read Song of Solomon 5:4. When have you experienced your heart pounding for your husband? Are you guilty of ceasing to think about your husband and more often thinking only about what he needs to do for you?

Apply

1. Identify one strategy you would like to put in place to help you move from making meat loaf to making love. Brainstorm together the details that this change of strategy would require.

2. Give each mom an index card and ask her to take two minutes to write down all the positive traits about her husband she can think of. Encourage her to keep it in her Bible or somewhere that will prompt her to thank God every day for one of her husband's wonderful qualities.

Pray

Have each mom thank God silently or aloud for the positive traits of her husband that she wrote on her card.

Ask God to help each of you make the mental and physical shift needed for lovemaking.

Praise God for being the Creator. Thank him for all that he has created, including physical intimacy.

Chapter Four: Intimacy Builders

Icebreaker

Ask group members to answer this question: When you were dating your husband, what was your favorite way to spend time together?

Dig Deep

1. Read Song of Solomon 7:10–12. How do these verses apply to the concept of dating? Discuss how God describes spending time together and even getting away for an overnight.

2. In conversation, what keeps you from focusing on your spouse's feelings or words? How does selfishness play a part in your lack of listening?

3. Read Romans 12:2. How does the world's concept of marriage differ from God's plan for the marital relationship? How can we "renew our minds" in regard to investing in our marriages?

Apply

1. Ask God to forgive you for any selfishness that has kept you from building intimacy in your marriage. Ask him to help you replace selfishness with selflessness in the future.

2. Ask your spouse about planning a marriage getaway. Discuss your budget, schedule, and possible itinerary for spending some time together. Be prepared to share your ideas with the group next week.

Pray

Pray specifically for each couple's dating schedule. Pray for God's wisdom on finances, schedule, and childcare. Ask God to lead the way.

Pray that each spouse would have a willing heart in spending time together.

Leader Assignment
If at all possible, try to get a copy of the song "Who Are You?" by Steve and Annie Chapman to play for the group next time you meet. It's on their CD *Kiss of Hearts* (www.steveandanniechapman.com/call.htm). If you can't find it, go back to page 103 and summarize it again for the group before the Dig Deep section.

Chapter Five: Who Am I? Mother or Lover?

Icebreaker
Have each person share what hobby or activity she enjoyed doing with her husband in their dating years before marriage.

Dig Deep
1. How did the idea presented in the Steve and Annie Chapman song challenge you? What can we learn from their song?

2. How do you and your husband work together as a team in parenting? Have you ever undermined him in front of the children? What impact does that have on your family dynamics? How does that affect the trust factor in your relationship?

3. Read Ephesians 5:31–33. This is the Bible's description of the "We are a team" mind-set. How does understanding this truth make a difference in your love relationship with your husband?

Apply

1. Identify and share three ways you can make a priority shift in putting your husband first.

2. Identify several heart issues that get in the way of making this shift (unforgiveness, anger, self-righteousness, pride, etc.). Commit to pray for one another this week on the issues you have identified in your discussion.

Pray

Thank God for the husband he has given to each mom in the group. Thank God you are not having to face parenthood alone.

Ask God to help you make daily decisions to be a wife first and mother second.

Leader Assignment

Bring in index cards and writing utensils to the next meeting.

Chapter Six: He's Not Wrong—Just Different!

Icebreaker

Ask participants to dream: If you could visit any country in the world, where would you go? Why?

Dig Deep

1. What is your love language? Give a specific, practical example of how someone could speak your love language.

2. What is your best guess at your husband's love language?

3. When looking at the eleven needs, what are your top three? Have you ever communicated these to your husband? Was he willing to identify his top needs? If so, were you surprised at all?

4. Read Romans 12:4–8. While this passage usually applies to the different gifts we are given within the church family, how can we apply this to our differences as husband and wife?

Apply

1. Have each mom write her husband's love language and top five needs on an index card. Encourage her to put the card in a place where she will see it regularly to remind her to step into his world.

2. What heart issues might get in the way of speaking your husband's love language or meeting his needs? Read Romans 12:17–20. How does this apply to a marriage in which one spouse is unwilling to serve and show love in actions? Have each mom share one heart issue (unforgiveness, pride, anger, self-sufficiency, etc.) that keeps her personally from affirming and encouraging her husband.

Pray

Thank God for the way he created us different from our spouses.

Praise God for his creativity when he knit us together in our mothers' wombs.

Ask God to help us move beyond the heart issues that keep us from affirming and encouraging our spouses.

Pray for open hearts as we continue this journey of self-discovery and learn more about God's plan for our marriages.

Chapter Seven:
What Are the Messages Only You Hear?

Icebreaker

Ask the women to describe a favorite hiding place when they were growing up. Do they have a place they get away to now? What is it?

Dig Deep

1. Read Proverbs 13:3 and 15:1. How do these verses apply to marriage? How does a gentle answer turn away wrath? What does this have to do with acting right even when a spouse acts wrong?

2. In learning to act in right, God-honoring ways, it is possible that we might go too far and begin to walk in pride. What kinds of thoughts about our husbands would we have if pride were in the picture?

3. Can you think of a time in the past two weeks when you might have wrongly interpreted a family member's behavior? How did you make it about you, when it really had nothing to do with you?

Apply
1. Identify and share a recurring message that only you can hear. Discuss each thought and offer suggestions to recognize and disarm the thought in the future.

2. Write down three positive statements about your husband that you can refer to when negative thoughts about him bombard your mind.

Pray
Ask God to help you recognize the damaging mental messages only you can hear.

Confess any time you've allowed the enemy to influence your thinking in the past week.

Thank God for his refreshing truths and our incredible value in him.

Leader Assignment
In preparation for the next discussion, take a look at the marriage seminars and retreats listed Appendix A. Find out if any will be located near you in the coming months. Be prepared to announce dates and information to the group.

Chapter Eight: Make the Marriage Investment

Icebreaker
Ask participants what their favorite class in high school was. Why?

Dig Deep
1. Have any of you ever been to a marriage seminar or retreat? What did you learn about yourself? Your spouse? Marriage in general? What benefits did you experience?

2. Have you ever thought about the need for marriage education? Brainstorm the benefits of attending an event every year or two.

3. Read Proverbs 23:12 and 19:20. What does God say will come from instruction and knowledge? How will that make a difference in marriage?

Apply

1. Identify the resources available in your community or in a nearby city. Discuss the possibility of attending an upcoming event as a group.

2. Discuss some other books about marriage that might be good to read as husband and wife, with blue and pink highlighters in hand. Consult Appendix A for suggestions.

Pray

Ask God to open the heart of each wife and each husband to making a marital investment.

Thank God for his word and the instruction we receive from it.

Leader Assignment

Bring index cards and writing utensils to the next meeting.

Chapter Nine: Sexual Differences: Don't Be Frustrated, Be Fascinated!

Icebreaker

Have each mom share her idea of a perfect romantic evening.

Dig Deep

1. Read Song of Solomon 5:10–16. Now read 7:1–9. How are the two descriptions similar? How are they different? In what way do these verses support the gender differences presented in this chapter?

2. What misconceptions can contribute to being frustrated by our differences rather than being fascinated by them?

3. Do you agree with the premise that sex begins in the kitchen? What causes you to feel physically drawn to your husband?

4. Can you think of a time you ignored your husband's need because you lacked an understanding of his difference as a man?

Apply
1. Pick one of your husband's sexual differences that you will choose to thank God for every day this week. In one or two sentences, write your prayer on an index card to remind you to thank God every day.

2. Encourage each mom to plan a date or a getaway time for her marriage. Has anyone already been working toward that goal? Share practical ideas that will help make the plan possible.

Pray

Ask God for forgiveness when you have not appreciated the unique way he has created your husband.

Thank him for making you uniquely female.

Ask God to help each mom work out the details to spend some alone time with her husband.

Leader Assignment

Ask all participants to bring a Bible to the next session. If women don't have Bibles, have some available. Also bring index cards.

Chapter Ten: Let Me Please You: Understanding the Concept of "Pleasuring"

Icebreaker

Have each mom finish this sentence: Just thinking about _____ brings a smile to my face!

Dig Deep

Open your Bibles to Song of Solomon. Take a few minutes to scan through the verses. Identify and then discuss references to giving or receiving pleasure.

Apply

1. Pass out index cards and ask the women to try to remember their wedding vows.

2. Try to put the vows in writing. Try to filter your thoughts about your sexual relationship through your wedding vows. Where have you made a promise you haven't kept? What vows have you successfully fulfilled?

Pray
Thank God for his promises to us. Praise him for being trustworthy.

Thank God for giving you, as a woman, the ability to receive sexual pleasure.

Leader Assignment
Bring paper, envelopes, and pens to the next meeting.

Chapter Eleven: Desire Details

Icebreaker
Have each mom finish this sentence: If I had twenty-four hours to use as I wanted, I would _____.

Dig Deep
1. Identify three ways you can prepare your mind for passion.

2. What have you learned about God in this study? What have you learned about yourself?

Apply

1. Read Song of Solomon 7:10–12. Paraphrase these verses in your own words. Personalize it if you want to.

2. Evaluate your love-making environment. Make a list of at least three things you can do this week to improve your environment for passion.

3. Distribute paper and envelopes. Ask participants to write a letter to themselves about all they have learned in this study. Have each person address an envelope to herself and seal the letter in the envelope. Collect the envelopes and mail them out in four to six weeks.

Pray

Thank God for the opportunity to be a part of this study.

Pray for each woman in the group, asking God to strengthen her marriage.

Once again, thank God for his wonderful gift of sexual intimacy!

Dear Reader,

THANK YOU FOR allowing me to share my heart and my stories with you. I hope this book has been helpful in your marriage journey. I'd love to hear your stories, your struggles, and your victories in marriage.

Please let me know what was helpful to you in the book. What would you like to hear more about? Did you use the Leader's Guide? If so, was it helpful? I look forward to your thoughts!

I can be reached personally by:

Mail: c/o Hearts at Home
            900 W. College Avenue
            Normal, IL 61761
Email: jillannsavage@yahoo.com
Website: www.hearts-at-home.org

My speaking schedule is posted on the Hearts at Home website—who knows, I might be coming to your area! If so, I'd love to meet you!

May God bless you on your marriage journey and may he always keep your heart at home.

Joining you in the journey,

Jill

Hearts at Home ®

The Hearts at Home organization is committed to meeting the needs of women in the profession of motherhood. Founded in 1993, Hearts at Home offers a variety of resources and events to assist women in their jobs as wives and mothers.

Find out how Hearts at Home can provide you with ongoing education and encouragement in the profession of motherhood. In addition to this book, our resources include the *Hearts at Home Magazine*, the *Hearts at Home Devotional*, and our Hearts at Home website. Additionally, Hearts at Home events make a great getaway for individuals, moms' groups, or for that special friend, sister, or sister-in-law. The regional conferences, attended by over ten thousand women each year, provide a unique, affordable, and highly encouraging weekend for the woman who takes the profession of motherhood seriously.

Hearts at Home
900 W. College Avenue
Normal, Illinois 61761
Phone: (309) 888-MOMS
Fax: (309) 888-4525
E-mail: hearts@hearts-at-home.org
Web: www.hearts-at-home.org

Would you like additional resources for your group?

We hope your moms' group has enjoyed reading *Is There Really Sex After Kids?* If you would like to enhance this learning opportunity by providing your group additional mothering resources, copy this page, fill in the information, and mail or fax it to Hearts at Home. Your sample resources (magazines, devotionals, and more!) are free of charge and will arrive within 3–6 weeks. (The form is also available on our website.)

Additionally, Hearts at Home maintains a comprehensive database of moms' groups in the United States. This allows us to operate as a clearinghouse for information about the groups. For instance, if a woman moves to a new community, she can contact Hearts at Home to locate a group in her area. If you would like to be part of the Moms Group Referral Network, please indicate below.

****

☐ Yes! Please send me resources for my group!

Please ship to _____

(Shipping address) _____

City _____ State _____ Zip _____

Contact name and phone number (___)_____

How many women regularly attend your group? _____

☐ Yes! Please include our group in your referral network!

Name of group _____

Meeting address _____

City _____ State _____ Zip _____

Contact name and phone number (___)_____

Contact email (if applicable) _____

Group website (if applicable) _____

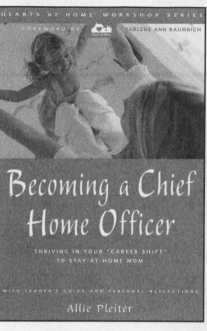

We want to hear from you. Please send your comments about this
book to us in care of the address below. Thank you.

GRAND RAPIDS, MICHIGAN 49530 USA

WWW.ZONDERVAN.COM